The
Money-Saving
Gardener

The
Money-Saving
Gardener

Create your dream garden
at a fraction of the cost

ANYA LAUTENBACH

CONTENTS

INTRODUCTION

I grew up surrounded by people passionate about nature, resourceful people who never wasted anything. Growing your own food and flowers wasn't a choice—it was a necessity to survive and stay sane. From a very early age I was taught self-sufficiency. We cared about the environment a lot, and I left home believing that nature—even the smallest insects—had the same right to be on this planet as we humans do. This approach taught me to see creating a garden as something that goes beyond the boundary of my own piece of land and my own needs, as a way of helping the planet.

My money-saving approach is a way to make stunning gardens in harmony with nature. Not only is the garden a refuge for nature, but it's created without spending a fortune. With the cost of everything going up, and the amount of disposable income being squeezed, gardens can seem like another thing that is out of reach, to be put on hold until times are better. I know that by sharing my knowledge I can make gardening and propagating more accessible, helping people create the garden of their dreams at a fraction of the cost of going out and buying what they need. It's possible to start now, and it's easier than most people think to make something beautiful without breaking the bank.

Propagation has been my passion for over 30 years. When I was a child, our windowsills were always packed with rooting treasures— my mother's cuttings. She got me into propagation when I was about 12 years old and showed me the satisfaction that comes with it. "Home is where your plants grow," she would say. When I started traveling as an adult, and felt unsettled, I realized she was so right.

A passion for propagation has helped me enormously on my journey, and I have never stopped propagating since I left home over two decades ago. When I was a young mother with a newborn and found myself away from home facing life's challenges, I came back to propagation as an easy, effective way to build up my garden. Inspired by the most beautiful garden created by my mother-in-law, I went back to my roots. My own garden captures the legacy of previous generations and my own passion, and looks to the future as my children become involved in it.

We've got to change how we garden, and I hope this book will be a great start for many people to achieve the garden they aspire to in a rewarding, affordable way.

CHAPTER 1

MAKE A START

Over the years, I have come to realize that the process of creating a garden is even more enjoyable and rewarding than the result itself. It is not about instant gratification or achieving one's goal, but rather about taking pleasure in the journey and, because nature can't be rushed, waiting is part of the process.

BUY LESS, WASTE LESS

My grandparents never wasted anything. I remember them saving pots and reusing all sorts of materials. This was before garden centers; instead, people like my grandparents simply used what they had, or what was given to them by friends and neighbors in return for something else. Even though she didn't have the most sophisticated equipment, my granny grew the most beautiful roses, dahlias, and lilies.

These days, gardening looks a lot different. It usually involves trips to the garden center to buy furniture, tools, and potting mix dug from peat bogs and sold in plastic bags. And plants—so many plants, often bought without considering whether they'll work in our garden. Then the tools break, the mix runs out, and the plants die because they needed different soil. So we head back to buy more.

While I've always been passionate about nature, and try to be environmentally conscious, like everyone else I'm not perfect. I used to use slug pellets, and I've only recently switched to peat-free potting mix. But when my boys came along, with their love for insects, birds, and all sorts of garden wildlife, I realized I had to do more to protect what they love. The way I choose to garden will have an impact on my boys' future, and I want to set a good example—just like the one my grandparents set for me.

Thinking differently

By choosing to buy less of what we don't have, and waste less of what we do, we can all act to make gardening more sustainable. This approach encourages us to garden in harmony with nature, to listen to the changing of the seasons by growing our plants from seed or by propagation instead of impulsively buying mass-grown bedding plants without knowing how to care for them or how long they'll last.

By gardening mindfully, I've come to appreciate how unnecessary most garden purchases are. Sure, you can find a plastic gadget for every purpose, but do you need it? The answer is: no, you don't! This doesn't mean I haven't spent anything on my garden. I still buy things; of course I do. But my favorite gardening tool is a dry beech stick that my son sharpened for me years ago. I use it to transplant seedlings and place cuttings in plant pots. It's truly multipurpose, and it was free.

The point is to think about what we really need to buy brand-new. If there's something I don't have that I genuinely need, I seek out quality pre-owned items online, or see what my local recycling center has to offer. The day I buy new plastic pots will be the day I'll stop gardening—which will never happen, because there are so many plastic pots already here on this planet. Buying more of them simply doesn't make sense: not for my bank balance, and certainly not for the environment.

Left Plants propagated from my garden, in secondhand pots.

TIME VERSUS MONEY

In gardening, as in many other areas of life, we often spend money to save ourselves time and effort. However, if you take a different approach—that is, spending more time and very little money—you may find that you not only save financially, but you're also rewarded with a sense of contentment and satisfaction you never thought possible.

Over the years, I have come to realize that the process of creating a garden is even more enjoyable and rewarding than the result itself. It is not about instant gratification or achieving one's goal, but rather about taking pleasure in the journey, and as nature can't be rushed, waiting is part of the process. A plant grown from a tiny speck of seed or a small cutting (see pp.110–59) will inevitably take longer to make an impact in the garden than a larger store-bought plant, but the anticipation and the sense of wonder you will experience when your flowers burst into life will be worth every minute of the wait. It is simply magical, and to me the journey is infinitely more engaging and rewarding than the more time-efficient one I make in my car driving to my local garden center!

Conscious buying

Even if propagating isn't for you, and you prefer to buy more established plants for greater impact in a shorter time, there are still many ways you can save money. Taking the time to really get to know your garden and think through your project before you act will have far-reaching results, both from an economic standpoint and in terms of success (see pp.16–17). You're more likely to choose plants that are suited to your garden, and

you'll get more out of them than your instant-impact purchases. Similarly, taking the time to really observe your existing plants and giving them a second chance—either in their current site or moving them somewhere else in the garden—will save you from buying more, possibly needlessly (see pp.22–23).

When it comes to buying containers, bear in mind you don't need to rush out and buy them all at once, and that they don't have to match, be brand-new, or even made for the purpose (see pp.30–31). It takes time to hunt around for pre-owned pots, but they are often more characterful than new containers, and when I find one that is "just right" for a fraction of the price, the sense of achievement I feel is far greater than I would get by simply clicking "Buy now."

The amount of time and money you're prepared to spend on your garden depends on your personal circumstances and lifestyle, but I believe the more time you put into your garden, and the more hands-on and self-sufficient you are, the more you'll get out of it.

Right To fill this border, I propagated the geranium and crocosmia, and grew this wonderful *Verbascum chaixii* from seed, instead of going out and buying all new plants.

LOOKING AHEAD

Before you start working on a new garden or making changes to an existing one, ask yourself what your priorities are. What role does your outdoor space play in your life and that of others who use it? How much time will you be able to dedicate to maintaining it? What is it that you want from your garden at this point in your life? And what are the next 10 or 20 years going to hold, if you're planning to stay in the same place? This will help you decide what to spend your time and money on.

These questions are not always easy to answer, but if you give them some thought it will help you focus on the budget for your projects. You will also avoid spending money carelessly, and be able to spend mindfully instead. There's no point in spending a lot of money on a project that will have to be removed in the next few years, or concentrating on one thing if there are other more important projects to do. Our houses and gardens adapt and evolve as our life progresses, so it's essential to be flexible while working toward your gardening goals.

Some people will think about making their garden suitable and fun for small children and pets. Some will want to focus on getting year-round interest out of the plants, or using their garden for entertaining, or as a sanctuary from busy surroundings.

For me a garden is an extension of the indoor space. I see it as a continuation of your style in the house, individual to you—not necessarily in a design-led way; more in a way of putting together colors and textures to

make a place where you feel happy. I tend to be quite eclectic and relaxed, but you might choose a minimalist garden style if that is how your house is, or an exuberant, colorful style. You can experiment and develop your own taste, building up your style instead of following gardening fashions.

Want versus need

There are crucial things that every garden will need. Just as a home needs walls and a general plan, your garden will need structure, and what comes with that are hedges, trees, boundaries, paths, a sitting area, and so on. If you are in an established mature garden, you might already have it all, but if not, it'll be up to you to decide about the future features of your garden.

I believe in keeping things simple and using your own resourcefulness to achieve the garden you want—even if it takes a bit longer. Explore what you have already (see pp.22–25), and focus on your needs rather than wants, then look at ways to obtain items and plants cheaply or for free (see p.30) to get a garden that's both affordable and unique to you.

Left A fort and climbing structure provides a focus for children amid the meadow and borders.

GETTING TO KNOW YOUR GARDEN

One of the most valuable things gardeners can do to reduce waste and save money is to take the time to really understand their garden. Only by watching and taking note of the conditions, from where the sunny spots are to what kind of soil you have, will you be able to choose the plants that will flourish year after year.

Imagine you've made a new friend and you're inviting them to dinner. Before they arrive, you'll probably ask them what they like to eat or if they have any allergies, so that you can prepare the right meal. If you didn't, and you served them something they hated or couldn't eat, your newfound friendship might not last that long. The same is true for plants and gardens. So often we bring home plants that look great without taking the time to learn their likes or dislikes, or whether our gardens will cater to their needs.

Aspect and soil type

Watch where the sun rises and sets in your garden; knowing which areas are sunny or shady is essential when it comes to choosing plants. Many plants require full sun, so there is no point in putting these in a shady corner of the garden and hoping for the best. They will struggle and may even die in just a few weeks. Instead, choose plants that actively like the shade—there are plenty of very beautiful plants that will thrive under a tree or in the shadow of a building (see p.18).

Similarly, knowing the type of soil you have in your garden is crucial to a plant's success. To identify your soil type, take a handful of soil and rub it between your fingers and thumb. If it feels sticky, damp, and heavy, it will have a high clay content and may become waterlogged easily. You should therefore avoid growing plants that require a light, well-drained soil, and opt for moisture-loving plants instead. If the soil feels loose and gritty or crumbly, it is probably sandy or chalky; these soils are very free-draining and are best suited to plants from hot climates, such as the Mediterranean, which are well adapted to drought and lack of nutrients (see p.73). In the middle of these two soil types is loam, which feels soft and even-textured, and is a mix of clay, sand, and silt. It holds moisture but is also free-draining, meaning that it doesn't become waterlogged. It's ideal for growing most plants.

In addition, some soils are more acidic, whereas some are more alkaline. This can also affect the plants you grow; a neutral soil supports the widest range of plants. If you are struggling to grow certain plants, do a soil pH test—kits are available from garden centers.

Gardening is not about what plants you want to grow but about choosing plants that will happily grow in your garden (see pp.18–19). By taking this flexible approach, you will save yourself a considerable amount of money as well as heartache.

First steps, clockwise from top left: taking note of details, such as these tiny hellebore seedlings growing in shade, helps you find out what grows in a garden and what the conditions are like; adaptable plants such as this *Geranium clarkei* 'Kashmir White' work in all sorts of conditions: exploring the soil to see what type it is—worms are a good sign; starting to add plants.

RIGHT PLANT, RIGHT PLACE

Once you have observed and understood the conditions in your garden, you can start to research plants that will thrive there. This gives you a freedom to try different plants, knowing that you are choosing ones that are likely to like the conditions you can provide.

Garden plants and houseplants all started as wild specimens from different parts of the world; many houseplants, for example, originated in humid jungle conditions or hot, dry deserts. Although the plants we buy and grow for our house and garden are less wild, and have been bred to make them more desirable and sometimes easier to grow, most retain their basic need for the conditions where they started.

Plants that are not suited to their conditions may grow initially, but will weaken, becoming more susceptible to attack by insects and diseases. Lavender, for example, originated in the rocky soil of the Mediterranean region and farther east. It needs free-draining soil and at least 6 hours of sunshine to perform at its best. If you plan to plant it in clay soil, you will first need to add lots and lots of sand to improve the drainage; otherwise, the roots will be cold and damp in winter, and the plant will be unlikely to thrive.

To find out about plants that may thrive in your garden, as a starting point notice what grows well in your local area. If there are other plants you particularly want to grow, perhaps ones you've seen in gardens farther afield, research them in gardening books and on websites to find out what they need to thrive, and whether you can provide it.

Changing the conditions

Sometimes you can change the conditions to suit the plant. If you really want to have lavender in a garden with clay soil, for example, plant it where drainage is better—in a raised bed, or a container of lighter potting mix. A tender plant such as agapanthus may not survive in a border, but if you grow it in a container, you can protect it from frost by keeping it near the house, or covering it in horticultural fleece if a very cold night is forecast. To grow Japanese maple (*Acer*) in a garden with alkaline soil, it might be best to plant it in a container of ericaceous potting mix (for acid-loving plants). So while you can adapt your garden to the plant, there are limits to what you can do.

Improving the soil (see pp.66–71) is always a good idea, and needn't be complicated or costly. For example, simply digging in organic matter, such as your own compost or well-rotted animal manure, adds nutrients and moisture-retaining body to dry soils, improves drainage of damp soils, and nourishes soil in shade.

Right Lavender and climbing roses in the sunny conditions that they love. **Overleaf** Two annual plants mingle well: blue love-in-a-mist (*Nigella damascena*) with purple annual sage (*Salvia viridis*).

HIDDEN TREASURES

If you've recently moved and inherited an overgrown,
unloved garden—or if you've been neglecting your own garden
and it needs some TLC—it can be tempting to rip out everything
and start again. Whatever you do, resist that temptation,
because with a little time and effort those untidy plants can
reveal themselves to be treasures in disguise.

Mature gardens are usually filled with hidden gems that may not be visible in the first few weeks or even months of your time in the new place. Your garden might be full of the most wonderful spring-flowering bulbs or flower seeds, which the preceding owners lovingly planted or sowed, yet these will remain buried below ground until they're exposed to warmth and moisture, which makes them spring into life and fulfill their potential. By not acting, you'll give nature a chance to reward you with its precious gifts—for free. Remember, you can easily divide clumps of bulbs and plant them elsewhere in the garden or in pots for some additional interest on your patio or garden table (see pp.140–41).

Some deciduous shrubs or trees that you inherit might seem like uninteresting-looking dry sticks in winter, but as the seasons change, the same plants may surprise you with their beauty. Shrubs and trees can take a long time to mature and can cost a lot of money to buy

Left The shrubs behind me, *Corylus* 'Red Majestic' and *Cotinus coggygria* 'Young Lady', may look bare in winter, but their color and texture are a treasure in the summer months.

as large plants, so don't be too hasty, and give them a chance to show themselves at their best before you consider getting rid of them.

As plants start to emerge, you can start to identify them and familiarize yourself with them, either by researching in gardening books or with a relevant app. Once you've identified the species or cultivar, you can research how to care for the plant and provide the ideal growing conditions to help it thrive.

Give plants a second chance

It's well worth giving garden plants that appear to be struggling a second chance instead of just disposing of them. For instance, if you have an old, neglected or straggly shrub, you can often restore it to its former glory by giving it a thorough prune. Before starting to prune, check the recommendations for pruning that particular species on a gardening website. Some plants respond better than others to drastic pruning, and it's important to get the timing right. Shrubs that can be easily rejuvenated by pruning include dogwoods (*Cornus*), common witch hazel (*Hamamelis virginiana*), spiraea, viburnum, and cotoneaster. It's safest to do a severe prune over a period of a few years, instead of cutting down the entire plant at once, which could kill it. Bear in mind you can use some of the stems as cuttings for creating new plants (see pp.114–35).

It is also worth digging up and moving plants if they aren't thriving in their current site (see p.84). Sometimes the issue is simply that the plant is in the wrong place—for example, it may need a sunnier or more sheltered position. Alternatively, the soil may be poor or not sufficiently free draining. If you improve the soil—by adding organic matter (see pp.66–69)—you may find that very soon the plant will grow in leaps and bounds. If you're not sure whether or not you want to keep a plant, but need to move it, plant it in a container until you decide. You can keep it in the pot, replant it elsewhere in the garden, or give it away to friends.

Transformations

If you have a large, mature tree that you find underwhelming, or even a dead tree, bear in mind that you can transform it by planting a rambling rose to scramble through and over its branches. You've not only saved the tree, which you might otherwise have had to replace at considerable cost, but it could become the highlight of your garden, for very little or no expense. Ideally, opt for a semi-evergreen rambler, such as rose 'Adélaïde d'Orléans' or 'Félicité Perpétue', which will provide interest throughout the year. When choosing a rambler, ensure you match the vigor of the rose to the tree; a strong, large tree makes a good support for a rampant rambling rose, while smaller trees can only cope with less vigorous ramblers.

Mature or dead trees are also excellent for wildlife, as food and shelter for insects, and as perches or even homes for birds, which in turn may feed on the insects. So your transformation may be saving and rejuvenating an important part of your garden's ecosystem.

Recycling your plants

Getting rid of plants should always be considered a last resort. If you do decide to dispose of them, ensure that you put your old plants on the compost heap so that they can be recycled as a soil conditioner. It's always best to shred woody stems and branches first because woody material breaks down very slowly and shredding helps speed up the process (see also pp.66–69).

Star plants, well worth keeping or moving, clockwise from top left: *Euphorbia griffithii* 'Fireglow' flowers in early spring, and self-seeds around the garden; crocosmia is easy to lift and plant elsewhere; branches of this *Viburnum plicatum* f. *tomentosum* 'Mariesii' root easily, creating new plants for free; this pink astilbe is easy to propagate by division and looks fantastic planted en masse.

MAKING CHANGES

At some point, you might want to make some substantial changes to your outdoor space. You might be creating a new garden from scratch or giving an existing garden a makeover. Before you embark on any major changes in a garden, take time to look at your options. Rushing often leads to costly mistakes, which cost yet more to rectify.

Think long term when making changes to your planting, and try to plan what you want to do and when. A lot of planting is best done in the winter, especially for shrubs and trees. For perennials it might be best to wait until the soil is warming up in spring.

Creating a new garden

If you're creating a new garden, you have the advantage of being able to plan and personalize the space. In a newly built house, the garden it comes with is very likely to contain poor soil, possibly filled with rubble and mortar. Digging some organic matter into your soil, and removing some of the rubble, will make a big difference and improve the soil's fertility and texture, without costing a lot (see pp.66–69). This means you are more likely to grow a greater number of plants that will thrive.

Filling the site with plants will invariably require more outlay than adding to an already established garden. To prevent your budget from getting out of control, consider your plant selection, and how you obtain the plants. Are you going to buy them new, or propagate them yourself (see pp.110–59)?

For quick impact and no cost, ask around friends or family and see if they could divide plants they have in their gardens and share the divided sections with you (see pp.136–41). And if you can't afford to buy larger shrubs

and trees, you can grow smaller specimens in pots for instant impact, then plant them in the ground later once they've grown.

After planting, it might look like there are huge gaps, and it can be tempting to add more plants. But remember that your plants will grow very quickly, and overplanting will be wasteful, as well as more work in the future.

Renovating an existing garden

If you have an established garden (either one you've just inherited or one you've had for a while), you may feel it's time for a change; perhaps it's overgrown, or you may have grown tired of it or dislike the preceding occupant's choice of plants. But don't be too hasty to remove plants; they may simply need a little TLC (see pp.23–24), and once they're gone you'll need to replace them. You may not have the time or money for taking on a major gardening project, but concentrating on one area—such a new border or even a container—can result in something wonderful. Perhaps you've got a few interesting plants that could be divided and planted in the new border or container to save you from buying new plants.

Right I bought this winter-flowering tree, *Prunus* x *subhirtella* 'Autumnalis Rosea' (here with lavender and *Hydrangea arborescens* 'Annabelle'), to celebrate the birth of one of my sons.

BEING RESOURCEFUL

If I need or want something for the garden, I never just go out and buy it. Instead, I first look around to see whether I already have something I could use as an alternative. I take great pleasure in thinking outside the box and making use of what's available. It's really satisfying to be as self-sufficient as possible—and it's a great money saver too, as well as better for the environment.

So much stuff has already been produced, and all those items are somewhere waiting to be found and reused. They might even be in your own garden if you take a closer look. Wood from old decking can be used to build compost bins and raised beds, old bricks can be used to build walls. My mother-in-law was my biggest influence when I was starting my gardening adventure. She used to have an area of her garden where she stored stone, old wood, old paving slabs, and a few other items for future projects. It really makes sense to put things aside if you have enough space, perhaps at the back of a shed, or in a corner screened by a large shrub. Later when you work on various projects, those items might be useful.

Before taking items to the recycling center or paying to have them hauled away, check whether you can use them. A rusty wheelbarrow could contain a summer display of flowers, or a piece of gutter could be a long container for shallow-rooted plants such as succulents or alpines. For many more ideas about repurposing containers, see pp.56–57. Sometimes things can just be left, and we can work around them; I have disguised an ugly shed by painting it dark gray and growing a climber up the side.

Using garden waste

Most gardens produce waste, but with very little additional work you can turn this waste into something useful and put it back into the garden. Buying a wood chipper is an expense (less so if it's second-hand), but in a larger garden with trees and shrubs, you will soon make your money back by using it to make wood chips to add to potting mix or use as a mulch. If you have large quantities, you can use it to make a wood-chip path.

All types of soil benefit from the addition of organic matter, and this needn't cost you a thing. Making compost (see pp.66–69) is an easy and environmentally friendly way of disposing of organic garden and kitchen waste, and provides a cost-free material that will greatly improve soil quality in your garden.

If you have old potting mix from pots where the plants are no longer needed or have been transplanted, you can add it to your compost heap, or you could reuse it right away for propagation because plants in the early stages don't need many nutrients.

Left I use prunings as supports for other plants, and sometimes for other projects (see pp.182–83).

SOURCING
SECONDHAND

People have been gardening for generations, and in the past communities often relied on one another to share items, instead of each household buying what they needed new. There is always bound to be someone who doesn't want something that you need. As the old saying goes, "One person's trash is another person's treasure." It's a win-win situation for everyone, including our precious planet.

I encourage everyone to ask their friends, family, and neighbors for items they need for their garden before buying anything. We live in such a busy world, and often people are keen to find a new home for items, but don't know where to start, particularly when they move or are carrying out renovation work. If they know you need an item, they may be happy to give it to you for free.

Social networking sites

Most areas have their own Freecycle website, where people offer unwanted items for free. You can also post a free "Wanted" ad there. The neighborhood social network site, Nextdoor, has a "Free Finds" page. Facebook Marketplace, Gumtree, and Preloved are similar, although people may be selling rather than giving away.

Recycling centers

I have always been a regular visitor to our local recycling center. In fact, most of my pots and containers come from there (see pp.56–57). The secret is timing! You'll compete with many gardeners in spring, and the best equipment will be quickly taken, but not many are interested in gardening equipment from mid-fall to winter. This is when the clever

money-saving gardeners step in. Some recycling centers where people drop off their household waste have a "reuse shop," where you can buy items that someone else no longer wants. The income often funds a charity or local community project. Every time I drop off my unwanted items, I have a quick look at the "new" unwanted stock. Unless a recycling center has such an arrangement, it's not permitted to just take items away.

Other sources

Car trunk sales can be good for pots, tools, and other items. Most areas have regular, large trunk sales, plus more local small-scale ones, all of which are worth a try. I find the more sales I go to, the more potential I can see in items—it's a skill that can be learned. Dumpsters may be full of interesting items that could be destined for landfill. Technically these belong to the person who threw them away until the dumpster is removed, and the dumpster is often on private land, so always ask permission if you're interested in anything.

Right These chairs, obtained free from a local group, look sharp with a coat of paint.

CHAPTER 2
SUPPORTING ACTS

Thinking about the bigger picture—how to organize your garden—can seem daunting. But if you work slowly and thoughtfully, there are plenty of money-saving ways to achieve the garden you want. From finding the right tools or making a wildlife-friendly boundary, to collecting gorgeous pots and furniture, you can create a garden that's individual and affordable, and works for you.

Tools that I wouldn't be without, clockwise from top left: a
selection of hand tools in a garden trug (basket) to keep them all
together; a garden spade; a warren hoe, for slicing through
weeds; a soil miller for breaking up the soil.

TOOLS

There are so many garden tools available, and it can be confusing to decide what's really needed and what's not. Every gardener needs tools, but when you start gardening you can create something amazing with just four tools, plus a watering can and a bucket. A little further down the line you can start adding more useful items to your collection.

For a start, the four tools that every gardener will need are a spade, a fork, a rake, and a hoe for weeding. If you're gardening only in containers, your list is even shorter: a hand fork and trowel. If you're buying from new, as with many garden-related products, the tools will be most expensive in the spring when everyone is thinking about getting back out into the garden. As a cheaper alternative, you can buy some great tools at a reduced price at the end of the growing season in late fall, or you may be able to find preowned ones on local Facebook or Freecycle groups. Although it's worth buying as good as you can afford in terms of quality, the main thing is just to buy (or borrow) what you need to get started.

As you become more serious about gardening, buying extra tools will make sense. Gardening tools are ideal to request as Christmas or birthday gifts, and it's worth mentioning them to friends and family who are looking for ideas.

Digging tools

Tools for cultivating include a spade, a digging fork, a hand fork, a trowel, a bulb planter, and a lawn-edging tool (see p.36). A bulb planter has a sharp edge for creating holes and is really useful in a large garden; you can also find hand bulb planters for smaller gardens—both are often reduced outside bulb-planting season.

Raking and weeding

For raking and weeding, there are several types of rakes. A garden rake (with a straight, rigid head) is useful when preparing the soil to sow seeds. A lawn rake (with a fan-shaped, more flexible head) is perfect to rake leaves for leaf mold, or rake moss out of your lawn.

For weeding there are various sorts of hoes, but one is enough—I recommend a warren hoe, which has a sharp, wide blade that cuts through weed stems. There are hand versions of some hoes, which are suitable for a small garden. A soil miller tool, which you roll over the soil to break it up to prepare it for planting, is another useful cultivating tool.

Other useful tools

This broad group of tools includes a wheelbarrow, watering cans, and other watering tools such as a hose, and a lawn mower. If you can buy a quality lawn mower, it's worth it if you have a reasonable area of grass. An electric mower works well in a smaller-sized garden, while a gas-powered mower is more practical for a larger one.

Some mowers have a mulching option, which is useful to cut the grass into short clippings that can be left on the lawn, fertilizing it and helping it stay moist, or for clippings that can be gathered and used as mulch (see pp.68–69).

For transplanting my seedlings, and lifting them from trays and pots, I use sticks found around the garden. I sharpen them to create my very precise little tool.

Cutting and pruning

For these tasks, I use pruners, precision pruners, lawn-edging shears, and battery-operated hand shears. You're unlikely to need all of these when you're getting started, but, depending on the sorts of tasks you do regularly, they can all be handy. Pruners are essential for pruning of all sorts, and I use precision pruners for more delicate jobs such as taking cuttings, cutting flowers, and deadheading. Battery-operated hand shears are more of an investment but save time if you have lots of hedges and lavender to trim. Hand shears are of course just as effective.

Looking after your tools

It's vital to maintain your tools well to make them last for years. Always remove the soil and put your tools away after finishing your jobs as rain will cause the wooden part to rot and metal elements to get rusty. From time to time, it's worth applying a little bit of linseed oil on the wooden handles. Getting a sharpening stone for your pruners and knives is a good idea; it's something my grandfather used to have, and I find it very useful too.

To avoid spending money on a tool rack, use a pallet attached to the wall of a shed to make a place to stand tall tools such as hoes, rakes, spades, and forks. Add strong hooks so you can store shears, trowel, and hand fork.

Anya's top tip

There are two tools I find transformational: a half-moon edging tool (below), and lawn edging shears. It's amazing what a difference they can make. I usually do my edging twice a year, in the spring and in the fall, making the garden look very neat. Even if your borders are wild and chaotic, having a cared-for edge makes your garden look crisp and inviting. I find that edging your borders is also a very therapeutic task, giving 100 percent satisfaction. It also makes an instant difference, unlike a lot of gardening tasks, which are all about slow nurturing.

Tools for cutting, and keeping tools in good condition, clockwise from top left: battery-operated hand shears; pruners; sharpening the blades of lawn-edging shears; applying linseed oil to the wooden shaft of a fork.

BEDS AND BORDERS

Creating a bed or border, whether in the ground or as a raised bed, is easier than It might seem at first. A beautiful, well-established border is not complicated to plant and maintain—although it does take some planning and taking care of.

A bed or border is a traditional way to group together plants to make a focused display. It's the most cost-effective option over a raised bed, but raised beds do have their place. They are neat and effective, offering deep, well-drained soil and easy access. As in a conventional border, you can grow almost any plants in raised beds, although vegetables and soft fruits are particularly popular.

Whether you're making a border or a raised bed, first assess the spot where you want to create it. Look at how much light and sunshine the area receives. If it is in shade for a large chunk of the day, take that into account when you plan your planting. Look at whether the soil is generally moist or dry (see also p.16). This way you'll have a better understanding of the conditions you can provide, and whether you might be able to improve the soil (see pp.66–71), and this will help you choose the plants that will thrive there.

Creating a border

Once you know the conditions you can provide, start planning and designing your border. You can use a piece of paper, your imagination, research, and common sense. Think of a border as a picture. Colors, shapes,

Left One of my borders in summer, full of perennials and a few biennials, with shrubs at the back.

and textures will contribute to your success. Remember to find out the ultimate size of your desired plants, so that you can give them enough space to grow and so that they don't overshadow each other.

If you are making a new border where you currently have a lawn, you can dig out the turf, turn it over, and cover it with fresh compost and soil. The grass under the ground will decompose and add more organic matter.

Your first stop for plants for your new border is your own garden. If possible, divide plants you have already and use the divisions to populate your new border (see pp.136–41). You can also move plants from one part of the garden to another. Later you can gradually add different plants (see pp.80–81 for lots of ideas of ways to obtain plants cheaply).

The main thing to remember when creating new borders is to continue looking after them until plants get established. Make sure you weed regularly, water the plants until they are growing well, and after that if it's dry, and continue edging your borders (see p.36) so that the grass does not grow into them.

Creating a raised bed

It's not surprising that raised beds are a popular choice in any size of garden. They allow you more control over the soil in which you are growing your plants. Because you can reach the whole bed from the edges, you don't need to stand on the soil to weed or plant in it, so the soil doesn't become compacted and it drains well. You can also top off with compost, so that the soil is rich and builds its fertility over time. If you want to plant acid-loving plants such as azaleas, heathers, and Japanese maples (*Acer*), but live in an area without acid soil, you could fill a bed with ericaceous potting mix for acid-loving plants, changing the soil pH in your bed. Because there is less bending down to care for plants in raised beds, they are also great for gardeners with mobility issues. Raised beds usually work best in a sunny spot where plants will receive plenty of light to thrive.

Allow for clear access from all sides of your raised bed. You will need space to care for your plants, water, weed, harvest, and, for annuals and some vegetables, clear your beds for the next growing season. Access for a wheelbarrow makes it easier for you to add some new potting mix or organic matter.

The first material that comes to mind for the sides of raised beds is wood. Wooden raised beds look fantastic, but because the wood is in direct contact with the ground and the soil inside, it will rot and need to be replaced after a few years depending on the type of wood you use. If you're buying new, choose wood treated with a preservative so it will last longer. Other more cost-effective materials are old bricks, or other building materials such as breeze blocks.

Buying direct from a DIY store is easy but probably the priciest option. You could contact local landscaping or building companies and get your materials at a more reasonable price. Sometimes asking among neighbors also produces great resources. Another, more creative, option could be modified furniture such as bed frames or chests of drawers, or even children's sandpits. They can be found on local Freecycle groups. Thinking outside the box instead of pressing the "buy now" button is always the most cost-effective solution.

When your raised bed is ready, you need to fill it. Instead of filling the whole depth of your raised bed with expensive new potting mix, you can choose another, more affordable way. About half of the depth of the raised bed can be filled with garden waste, such as small, fine branches, leaves, grass cuttings, and anything that will happily rot away. The remaining half can be soil from your garden, or bought in specially, mixed with organic matter such as well-rotted manure or compost.

Every spring you can add extra manure or sow some green manure (see p.70) to improve the quality of the soil. A pack of green manure seeds will only cost you a couple of dollars and will take just a few minutes to sow. It's a fantastic way of adding extra nutrients for your plants to thrive in the coming months.

Rejuvenating an overgrown bed

If your border has become shaggy and congested, start by edging the border to reestablish its shape, and make it look crisp. Weed the soil and add some fresh soil and organic matter such as compost. Overgrown, mature perennial plants should be divided every few years (see pp.136–39), and the divisions replanted with space to grow; this will rejuvenate them. Overgrown shrubs should be pruned (see p.84). Always check the ultimate size of shrubs and don't plant them too close to other plants to avoid constant pruning. Aim to keep the border weed-free to allow other plants, especially young ones, to get established.

Right I plant seedlings of annuals, such as cosmos, to fill any gaps in my herbaceous border.

A path or patio doesn't need to be a bare expanse: it can connect with the rest of your garden. Here a lupin seedling is growing in my gravel path. Sometimes I allow seedlings to develop to soften the look of the path, and sometimes I transplant the seedlings to a more suitable place.

PATHS AND PATIOS

One of the main ways of organizing the space in your garden, paths and patios can divide your garden into different zones while creating interest and places to linger. They work best if they are long-lasting and low maintenance, and can be created from all sorts of materials. Hard landscaping can be expensive, but there are more cost-effective alternatives.

Paths lead you to other areas of your garden, and used well, they offer a promise of something new, a surprise. Different areas of the garden are used more or less frequently, and paths ideally connect the most-used features, such as the vegetable bed, the compost heap, or the sunny seating area at the end of the garden. They can be ornamental as well as practical, both in the route they take and in the materials used to make them.

Adding a new patio can be a bigger investment, but there are ways to save money. Think carefully about where you want to spend time sitting in the garden. A tiny area with a table and a few pots outside your back door can be a great place to sit, or you may choose a spot at the end of the garden to watch the sunset. This is a decision to make over time as you get to know your garden and how you want to use it.

Creating a path or patio

You may decide that you want to invest in building a good path or patio as a permanent part of your garden's infrastructure. But if you don't want to hire a landscaping company that will use more conventional materials and will cost a lot of money, you can create a path yourself from all sorts of different preowned and recycled materials. For fairly low-traffic areas, paths can be made from materials such as roof tiles, rocks, various elements of dismantled decking, logs, pieces of an old fence or even broken pottery. Old paving slabs can form a hard-wearing path or patio, and you can space them apart with gravel in between to save on costs (see "Edges and gaps," overleaf).

It can be harder to find the quantities of paving that you may need for a patio. If you can find some second hand online, take into account delivery costs and logistics: stones are heavy to transport. Asking locally saves on the longer-distance costs.

Research how to lay your patio or path, whatever material you use, and ensure you take into account drainage so that water doesn't sit on the surface but runs off into the garden (rather than toward the house).

Sources of materials

If you have some "behind the scenes" space in your garden, such as the back of a shed, I highly recommend that you store old or leftover paving slabs, bricks, roof tiles, and even old pottery. Those items can be also found online or locally among neighbors or friends. Remember: one person's trash is another person's treasure. Landscaping companies might be another good source for buying unwanted leftover materials and saving a lot of money. Not everything has to be matching. Sometimes mixing materials can create an interesting effect. Searching for ideas on Pinterest and other social media platforms can be truly inspirational.

Edges and gaps

To make your path or patio less formal, to soften the edges, and to make moving around the garden a more exciting experience, you can grow interesting ground cover or creeping plants. They will create a dense carpet that will not only happily grow between the paving slabs or gravel, but at the same time suppress the weeds and save time on weed control. You can even lay paving slabs with wider spaces between them (reducing the number you need to buy), and fill the gaps with low plants. To add more ground cover instead of spending more money on hard landscaping will also be beneficial for your local wildlife, which will positively contribute to the biodiversity of your garden and save on pest control.

Low-growing, spreading plants to soften the edges include creeping Jenny (*Lysimachia nummularia*), low-growing phlox (*Phlox douglasii* 'Crackerjack', or *Phlox subulata* 'Snowflake'), creeping mazus (*Mazus reptans* 'Blue'), or Mexican daisy (*Erigeron karvinskianus*). Most are easy to propagate (see pp.122–25), so you could buy a few and then take cuttings and raise your own to fill the spaces. If they start to spread too far, just cut them back—and you many be able to use the trimmings to make more plants.

Allowing mosses and lichens to slowly colonize your paving will also help it blend in with the rest of the garden.

Rethinking what plants can do

There are many alternatives to hard landscaping. Instead of paths made from expensive materials, you can simply cut paths in your lawn, leaving areas of long grass, and creating wavy walkways leading to a focal point. It's an instant-impact result that will give you a sense of achievement and will not involve any money. That focal point could be a neatly cut grassy area where you could place a large planter or a bench found on a local Facebook group. This way you'll also create different textures that change through the seasons, and the long grass will add movement. But do be aware of any restrictions on long grass from your homeowners' association.

Maintaining paths and patios

In my eyes, a natural garden is the most beautiful, so I'm not a fan of power washing patios or paths. However, it's a good idea to trim back plants if they are encroaching too far and making the path slippery. And if paving slabs are wobbly, check and adjust them, or lay them again so that they are safer to walk on.

Right A mowed grass path forms an enticing walkway.

A range of boundaries, clockwise from top left: an informal hedge of *Hydrangea arborescens* 'Annabelle'; a beech hedge grown from plants reduced in price in an end-of-season sale; morning glory growing on a support to add interest to a wall; a yew hedge, evergreen for maximum privacy, and not as slow-growing as it's reputed to be.

BOUNDARIES

The edges of your garden, as well as areas within it, often need to be clearly defined. Fences and hedges are popular options, offering different levels of privacy and protection, and varying widely in price.

The most cost-effective fences and hedges are those that are already there. So for the money-saving gardener the first stop needs to be mending or renovating what you have.

Fences

Offering a solid barrier that often lasts for years and can also support plants, fences take up minimal space, and so they make a good boundary for a small garden. If the fence doesn't look good, it can be sanded and painted to give it a new lease on life. Sometimes a leaning fence will only need a few new posts or a replacement panel. If you think you may need to replace a fence, get some professional advice to check whether it can be fixed instead.

You can plant climbers to cover an unsightly fence (or just to bring more flowers into the vertical spaces; see also pp.96–97). A very good source of information is the RHS website, where you can select the aspect you've got and there'll be a list of suitable plants. Bear in mind that some climbers are very vigorous and might damage a wooden fence in the long term. Some roses, climbing hydrangea, and clematis are beautiful additions to a fence. Climbers offer places for birds to roost or nest, and insects to feed. This can counteract one of the downsides of fences: because wildlife can't move easily between spaces where there is a solid barrier, you may need to spend more money or time on pest control if animals can't access your garden. To remedy this, cut a small arch in the base of the fence to allow movement across the boundary.

Hedges

A hedge might last longer than a fence and will not only be cheaper, but also more environmentally friendly, creating habitats for birds and insects. Wildlife will have good access to your garden through a hedge.

The most economical way to start a new hedge from scratch (or to replace a fence) is to buy your hedging plants bare-rooted when they are very small, or in plant sales. A lot of hedging plants such as beech, privet, laurel, and hawthorn can also be propagated, so if you know that in a few years' time there's a fence that needs replacing, it's a good idea to raise some new plants. Hedges need annual pruning to keep them bushy.

Another cost-effective solution is a "dead hedge"—a barrier in the shape of a hedge made from garden material such as pruned branches, foliage, and materials from clearing the garden. These twiggy growths are laid flat and held in place by vertical stakes. Because you'll only use materials available from your garden, a dead hedge won't cost you anything—apart from the cost of the strong stakes if you don't have them already. A dead hedge can also be a temporary solution to create privacy while a new hedge is growing. It makes a wonderful habitat for a lot of wildlife such as birds and useful bugs.

PLANT SUPPORTS

Support is incredibly important for climbers, roses, and taller perennials such as dahlias or peonies, allowing the plant to look its best for many months. Effective support doesn't have to cost a lot, and can look beautiful in its own right.

Support works best when it is put in place in advance—before the plant really needs it—and when it suits the vigor of the plant being supported. Without staking, plants can be damaged by the wind and rain. This means thinking ahead. When I prune trees, shrubs, and hedges, I keep all the branches for supporting my plants. I like the natural look of local wood instead of bamboo, and using what you grow feels good. If you haven't got any trees or not enough, contact local coppicing companies to see if you can buy your plant support from them.

I always start staking my plants in very early spring before the leaves emerge, so that nothing gets damaged and the plant can grow through and over its support. By midsummer all my plants are well supported, and don't need much of my attention, but I keep some branches through the year in case a plant needs extra support.

Creating wooden supports

Making my plant supports has become a ritual in my garden, both useful and satisfying. Many years ago, when I was designing our garden, I visited others for inspiration. In winter and very early spring I could see public gardens from a different angle. It felt like I was seeing them behind the scenes. I also had free demonstrations on how to professionally create a plant support; people are so friendly, and gardens aren't busy early in the year, so I was able to ask questions about the types of branches they use and simply watch and learn.

When we prune our beech hedges, I trim the branches to about 8–10in (20–25cm) long and use them to support my sweet-pea seedlings and some spring flowers, such as hydrangeas, in containers. I make a sloping cut at the base, so they are more easily pushed into the pots. For stronger supports for taller perennials, such as dahlias and gladioli, I find birch or hazel are best. Their branches can be woven into domes or obelisks (see pp.166–69) because they are bendy and don't even need twine to secure them. It's best to avoid using branches from willow or dogwood because they root easily.

Other supports

Plant support is also available as metal frames. I don't recommend using plastic, but I do use metal rings to support peonies and hydrangeas, placing them in early spring for the new shoots to grow through. Many ornamental grasses and more compact varieties of herbaceous perennials don't need any support at all, so it's always good to include them in your garden because they can simply take care of themselves, and often act as extra support for nearby plants.

A variety of supports, clockwise from top left: one of my handmade birch and hazel supports for *Clematis viticella* 'Etoile Violette'; a tripod for annual climbers such as sweet peas; *Nepeta* 'Six Hills Giant' growing through its support; a woven dome structure for plants to grow through.

LAWNS AND MEADOWS

Lawns are great, but meadows are better. It's my view that immaculate, weed-free lawns are a thing of the past. Meadows are not only better for wildlife and the environment, but also for our pockets.

If you're not quite ready to give up your lawn yet, it's possible to combine both lawn and meadow, or to transition gently from one to another, even in a small garden.

Lawns

To have a perfect-looking lawn it's necessary to invest money and time. Products to feed the grass and to kill weeds and moss are expensive and not environmentally friendly. If you do decide to create a lawn, I highly recommend that you let some other plants grow in it instead of killing them. Commonly known as "weeds," those plants are your good friends.

As summers are getting hotter and drier, and water and energy costs are rising, it's more difficult and sometimes impossible to keep a traditional lawn looking green. Letting lawns grow slightly longer allows them to stay greener as they hold onto more moisture in the ground, and the grass has deeper, more effective roots. Longer grass is also more wildlife friendly.

As a halfway house you could introduce stripes of longer grass to separate different areas of your garden. In these longer areas, you can plant some spring-flowering bulbs such as daffodils, alliums, and camassias. This will only involve a few packets of bulbs, but is a high-impact solution, easy to create and very cost-effective too.

Clover lawns

As an alternative to a conventional lawn, if your HOA allows, you could try a clover lawn. White clover (*Trifolium repens*) not only looks great, but it's also more drought tolerant than grass, which means that it'll stay green all summer with a minimum amount of water. Clover is one of the most common lawn plants, and can create a sea of white flowers. It is also a natural fertilizer as its roots "fix" nitrogen from the atmosphere, then when the clover loses leaves or its roots die, the nitrogen enters the soil. Clover will need less mowing, which will result in less gas or electricity used for your lawnmower, and less time spent cutting the lawn. In fact, it only needs mowing once a year in late summer after self-seeding. White clover will not need any fertilizers and will outcompete other weeds. It can grow in poor soil, so there's no need to invest in expensive topsoil.

White clover flowers attract many friendly insects including parasitoid wasps. Despite their unappealing name, these tiny wasps feed on aphids and other garden pests and they are the most useful insects a gardener could have.

To establish a clover lawn, in some cases all you need to do is stop using weedkillers

Right Self-seeded oxeye daisies and other flowers that appeared in our meadow after leaving it unmowed.

and let nature take over. White clover prefers clay soils, and will often start growing and self-seeding in your lawn without any additional costs. You can also buy seeds and sow them in a bare patch of lawn in spring. Make sure that you let your white clover self-seed because this plant is a short-lived perennial. Don't use any weed killers on your lawn; they'll kill the clover.

Meadows

Having a meadow creates interest and, if you let nature take over, you might end up with some exciting surprises such as native wildflowers, gorgeous textures, and a range of colors. All of that with very little money spent. Even the smallest space can have an area where you allow in wild plants.

One way to create a wildflower meadow is to buy and sow wildflower seeds and plants, but this can be expensive. If you don't want to spend much money but still have a wonderful meadow, you can basically let it be!

The idea behind changing from a lawn to a meadow is to let all the native wildflowers appear on their own. At first the grass will dominate and may crowd out the wildflowers. This is where a fabulous annual native plant comes in: yellow rattle (*Rhinanthus minor*). It is semi-parasitic and will feed off the grass roots and eliminate grass from the area. Sowing yellow rattle is a very cost-effective way of turning your lawn into a meadow—even better if you collect your yellow rattle seeds on your walks at the end of the summer. (see p.157) Always ask the landowner's permission, or if you are collecting from a public place, ensure it is not a protected site, and only collect if there is lots to spare—you won't need many. As the name suggests, the seeds are easy to identify because they make a rattling sound when you touch their seed pods. They can be found in wildflower meadows around the countryside.

After introducing yellow rattle, you can watch your flower meadow evolve, and it's the most fascinating thing. As the grass starts disappearing, some native wildflowers will start to thrive within the first year. At the end of the summer after all the plants have set seed and the seeds have self-sown, cut the meadow and let the process start again.

Anya's top tip

The most important thing when creating a wildflower meadow is to keep the soil nutrient poor. When you cut the grass at the end of the summer, remove the trimmings so that they don't break down and add nutrients to the soil. Never use fertilizers because they will stimulate the growth of grass at the expense of wildflowers.

Wilder grassy areas, clockwise from top left: a bumblebee feeding on white clover; *Allium hollandicum* 'Purple Sensation' in the wildflower meadow, adding early summer color; yellow rattle in midsummer with some flowers still in bloom and seeds forming in their pods; naturalized daffodils in the meadow in early spring.

A mixture of oxygenating plants under the water and taller plants that float on the water or grow out of it can create a balance, keeping the pond healthy; when some light can reach the depths of the pond, oxygenators can work to keep your pond clean.

PONDS

Where there's water, there's life. Adding any type of pond to your garden will attract wildlife and make your garden more biodiverse, as well as more interesting. Wildlife such as birds and friendly insects will help with controlling less welcome insects, saving time and money.

It's possible to create space for water even in the smallest garden, without spending too much money. All you need is a large container that will hold water; it can be an old bath, sink, or even half a whiskey barrel. If there are holes in it, you can always use a pond liner to cover them (available from most garden centers or DIY stores). Here I am focusing on smaller ponds that are easier and cheaper to achieve.

A larger pond is more of a project, and can be costly—but if that is what you want to have, it's worth doing your research to plan and create it properly, and it will repay your care.

It's important to mention that even the smallest pond can be dangerous, so if there are children visiting your garden, make sure you keep them safe.

Siting your mini-pond
A water feature in a container can live anywhere in your garden—on the patio or in the vegetable plot, or in a spot where it will act as a focal point, a destination to walk to, to stop, and to observe nature. If you prefer you can dig a hole and place your container in the ground.

You need to establish your mini-pond in a level spot, preferably away from trees and shrubs so that leaves don't fall into the water. You're looking for a mixture of sun and shade. Before you fill the container with water, place some rocks inside to make it easy for wildlife to climb in and out. Rocks and even logs can look very attractive mixed with plants and water. Carefully fill the pond—using rainwater if you have it—without dislodging the stones.

Planting and maintaining
The next step is to make sure that the water in your mini-pond stays clean. The natural, most cost-effective way to do this is by using oxygenator plants. These plants grow underwater, producing oxygen during the day, keeping your pond clean, and minimizing algae, which grow and spread in conditions where there is little oxygen, sometimes covering the whole surface of the water if unchecked. Some oxygenator plants such as water violet (*Hottonia palustris*) or water crowfoot (*Ranunculus aquatilis*) will also flower, adding extra interest to your pond, and attract pollinating insects. Other excellent choices are willow moss (*Fontinalis antipyretica*) and hornwort (*Ceratophyllum demersum*). Now you can also add some other pond plants, such as water poppy (*Hydrocleys nymphoides*).

Check water levels in a dry spell and top off if needed. Pull out leaves that fall into the water in fall. From time to time you may need to pull out some of the weed if your pond is becoming overcrowded. It's good to have at least one third of your pond surface clear.

A variety of containers, clockwise from top left: a colorful can makes a striking container for growing a seedling; small bottles display delicate flowers including love-in-a-mist (*Nigella*); drainage holes drilled in an old whiskey half barrel; sweet peas in an old kitchen jug.

POTS AND CONTAINERS

Whether they are for plant displays on your terrace, or to hold precious cuttings as they develop roots, pots and containers are a key part of developing and growing any garden. Fortunately they are relatively easy to pick up cheaply and you can build up your collection slowly.

The more imaginative and prepared to improvise you are, the more money you can save. Whenever you see interesting ideas, make a note of them, or take a quick photo to bear in mind for later projects. If you need suggestions for what to plant in your improvised containers, it's well worth looking at Pinterest or Instagram for inspiration.

Repurposing containers

Unwanted items can make perfect planters. For example, a farmhouse sink, or a zinc trough or bucket, filled with forget-me-nots or spring-flowering bulbs can look fantastic, and later in the season they can be replaced with foxgloves, dahlias, and other cottage-garden plants. Other possibilities include a rusty can planted with succulents or saxifrage, or a pair of worn-out garden boots, a leaky watering can, or even an old tea kettle filled with cascading plants, such as creeping Jenny *(Lysimachia nummularia)*, which can cover imperfections. An old bathtub is perfect for edibles such as strawberries or cherry tomatoes, both hungry plants.

Containers don't always need to be deep, provided you select plants carefully. Plants with very shallow root systems, such as sedums or sempervivums, can grow in the most unusual containers such as large seashells.

Whatever you decide to adapt, drill some drainage holes in the bottom so that the soil doesn't become waterlogged. I usually drill one to five holes, spaced 2–3in (5–8cm) apart, depending on the size of the container.

Making a display

You can find creative ways to display containers too. An old chair can be attached to a wall to make a shelf for pots. A ladder can form layers of shelving for small containers. An old cart filled with pots and positioned near a table and chairs allows you to enjoy plants at closer range when you sit in the garden. Don't forget to look out for containers for cut flowers too: decorative old bottles and jars work well, or sometimes cracked or chipped china.

Unwanted pots

I used to buy plastic pots for propagation, but I quickly realized how unnecessary this was. There are so many plastic containers already, which people don't want—I just needed to find my way to them. I contacted some landscaping companies, and they gave me hundreds of unwanted pots that I keep reusing. I also use fruit containers from the supermarket or egg boxes for seedlings. The cardboard centers of toilet paper rolls are great for sweet pea seeds, which like a deep, narrow container.

GARDEN FURNITURE

You can transform your outdoor space into a green living room with spaces to relax, entertain, or even use as an alternative place to work. Finding furniture at a reasonable price is entirely possible and can enable you to create an inviting and unique area.

Adding furniture to your garden will encourage you to spend more time outside and give you an opportunity to really enjoy your space. Garden furniture can be also used cleverly to enhance your garden by creating focal points. It's possible to introduce a lovely, eye-catching element or some carefully chosen color by adding, for example, a preowned bench next to a large planter or a group of planters at the end of the path, or a brightly painted bistro set in the afternoon sun with some interesting succulents in a pot on the table. Furniture placed away from the house will also give you an opportunity to stop, sit down, and observe the house and garden from a different perspective.

Finding the right furniture

Not all furniture needs to be matching. Mixing wood with metal or rattan, hanging chairs and hammocks, individual chairs, and stools can create a lovely and relaxing outdoor space. But how can you find the right furniture at a reasonable price?

Many items of furniture can be made out of recycled materials, and some people are very creative at making their own. If you want to buy some new garden furniture, choose your timing wisely. Furniture companies know exactly when people start thinking about their outdoor spaces, and that's when the garden furniture will be at its most expensive. Try to think ahead and buy your garden furniture out of season—perhaps in late summer or fall—it will save you a lot of money. If you're prepared to buy second-hand furniture, it makes sense to look for it in the winter and spring when people replace their furniture and get rid of the old. This is where you could be looking at preowned or freecycle online groups, or even local recycling centers that have stores.

Whether your furniture is new or preowned, consider what type of material your furniture is made of to make sure your investment is worth your money. I wouldn't advise buying new plastic furniture, but you could consider second-hand pieces. Metal and wood can be long-lasting if preowned—make sure they are sound before buying them, though. Then take care of your furniture, cleaning and oiling or painting wooden furniture, and sanding and repainting metal items. If you have space, keep the furniture undercover in winter so that it's out of the worst of the elements.

Right If you maintain your furniture with care, it should last you for many seasons.

CHAPTER 3
THE NATURAL GARDEN

It's our choice what we do in our gardens, how much money we spend, what we grow, and how much we care about the environment. One thing is sure: living in harmony with nature saves money.

WORKING IN HARMONY WITH NATURE

In gardening there are many routes to success. I always like to work with the environment and wildlife while still enjoying the process and the final result. Working in harmony with nature not only saves time and money, but also makes the gardens of our dreams more achievable.

Every element of the food chain in our garden is vital, and the less we intervene, the more will be achieved. As a beekeeper with a huge passion for pollinators, I like my garden to be as wildlife friendly as possible. The more insects and animals, the merrier. Of course there will always be slugs, snails, and caterpillars in your garden, but you need them to feed the birds (and frogs if you're lucky). If there is a balance of wildlife, pests become less of a problem. If you take out one part of the garden ecosystem, other parts can't survive: your garden is poorer in wildlife and less resilient.

Maximize wild habitats

What's the secret? We've got to start with providing as many habitats for wildlife as possible. This will encourage natural predators, such as birds, frogs, ladybugs, toads, centipedes, ground beetles, and more. They eat slugs and aphids. Also vital for a healthy garden ecosystem are nutrient-rich soil (see pp.66–71) and healthy, robust plants. Together these elements of good soil, abundant wildlife, and strong plants support and sustain each other, making your garden more successful, and

Left Lavender attracts a huge variety of bees and other pollinators.

enabling it to withstand adverse events. With increasingly extreme weather, it's essential to give your garden the best chance you can for it to flourish and adapt (see pp.72–73).

Leaving grass longer

Leaving some areas in your garden unmowed (if your neighborhood allows) is the simplest and best single thing you can do to make a difference. Areas around trees, or at the edges of your garden are easy to leave, and if millions of gardeners let an area of their garden remain untouched, it could provide food and homes for millions more wild creatures. Let it be as natural as possible, only cutting that wild area once a year toward the end of the summer, so that all the plants growing there have set seed. Observe and listen to that part of your garden to get to know the wild visitors and which plants they like. Dandelions will provide food for pollinators, and stinging nettles will be food for caterpillars of butterflies such as peacocks, small tortoiseshells, and commas. Insects are the base of the food chain, and if they can't survive, everything else suffers.

On a larger scale, wildflower meadows can be truly amazing (see pp.50–53). But even in a smaller garden you can have a little wildflower patch, or convert your lawn and mow in a path. The textures that wild areas will add in your garden can be breathtaking. Working in harmony with nature is a win-win for all!

Companion planting

If we plant rows or blocks of the same plants, we are creating the ideal conditions for certain insects or diseases to move freely from one plant to the next. They will quickly increase in number, and their scale will soon cause a problem. For example, lots of cabbages in a block are likely to attract cabbage white butterflies to lay their eggs; their caterpillars will munch through a lot of leaves. It may take time and money to get the problem back under control—and you may be tempted to resort to costly and harmful chemicals.

An alternative approach is to break up the rows or blocks of cabbages with other plants such as nasturtiums, which will attract the butterflies away, helping keep damage to cabbage leaves to a minimum. This is known as companion planting, which is a method of combining plants that are beneficial to each other. The plants form two elements of an ecosystem that allows them to grow more strongly together and be less susceptible to potential attack from insects and diseases. Companion planting with flowering plants is also a great way of attracting much-needed pollinators. Mixing strongly scented ornamentals with edibles can help deter pests, protecting crops and saving money.

How you do this depends, of course, on which plants we are talking about. If we use perennials such as lavender or sage as companion plants, it works to just leave them where they are and plant other plants next to them. For annuals such as nasturtiums, you would need to start them from seeds or seedlings every year and plant them outdoors at the same time as the other plants that need protection, such as tomatoes. Some popular and effective combinations are: ornamental alliums with carrots; thyme with roses; lavender with rosemary; borage with strawberries; pot marigolds (*Calendula*) with zucchini; French marigolds (*Tagetes patula*) with tomatoes; and nasturtiums with cucumbers.

Avoiding chemicals

Using pesticides and fungicides means that you not only kill the "pests," but also harm other vital elements of the ecosystem, causing more damage, which may lead to spending more money. Chemicals should be a distant memory for us all! Mulching instead of using weed killers has been successful for me (see pp.68–69). I also let fallen leaves remain on the soil over the winter to suppress weeds.

If you are tempted to use a quick (and costly) fix and apply a chemical pesticide, think again. You will also be killing all of the insects that feed on "pests," as well as beneficial insects such as bees, moths, and butterflies that pollinate your flowers, and make the garden such a joyful place to be. Also, as I mentioned above, removing one type of wild creature creates an imbalance, and others move in, or move out, which may cause problems further down the line. Working with nature rather than against it is the key.

Right A marbled white butterfly enjoying the meadow grasses.

IMPROVING
YOUR SOIL

Soil is the foundation of your garden's health, but there's no need to go out and buy expensive additives to improve your soil. By working in harmony with nature, you can see your garden as a "shopping center" for gardening materials: you can use what you already have. This also keeps nutrients within the garden's ecosystem, so that the garden benefits from your hard work and the help of the wildlife that visits.

There are various ways to replenish and protect your soil. Making and adding compost will provide nutrients that plants can access as they grow, as well as improving the texture of the soil. It's also important to protect your soil from water loss, and to enable it to regulate its temperature: a mulch on top of the soil will help with this (see pp68–69). For ways to fertilize your soil naturally, see pp.70–71.

Making your own compost

Making your own compost can become a bit of an obsession. The end result you are looking for is beautiful, dark, and crumbly, ideal for mulching and enriching your soil. In most gardens, there is space for a compost heap or some form of compost bin. You can make a heap in a corner, or use pallets to create a compost bin, or buy one of the many types that are for sale. Sometimes local agencies offer compost bins at a reduced price or free—and they will even deliver them.

Your compost bin needs to be in an accessible place so that you easily put in waste and hopefully shovel out compost to use. You might not want to have it visible, though—see if you can find a slightly tucked-away spot. If possible, put it in partial shade so that it doesn't get too warm or cold. You don't want it to dry out or get waterlogged, either. But don't worry too much; there's no "perfect" position, and a heap may just take slightly longer to decompose if it's not in the optimal place.

What to add to your compost bin

Making compost is a good way to reduce your kitchen waste, make use of your garden waste, and even reduce your recycling. It's hard to be precise about what you need to make good compost, but you're aiming for roughly half nitrogen (green) and half carbon (brown). The nitrogen additives can be from grass cuttings, annual weeds, vegetable and fruit peelings, coffee grounds and tea bags, plants that you have cut back, and deadheaded flowers. The carbon-rich additions to your heap can be dead leaves, chopped up twigs and branches, shredded cardboard and paper, old straw, sawdust, and ash from wood fires. Avoid putting any cooked food on the heap because it may attract vermin.

With the correct balance of materials all mixed up, the bacteria and microorganisms can break them down to form compost in a few months. Turning the heap from time to time will help to get in air to speed up the process.

Adding nitrogen-rich green garden clippings to my compost bin. I balance this by adding some carbon-rich waste, such as shredded cardboard because lots of green waste, especially grass clippings, can get slimy if it's not mixed with other types of materials.

Perhaps you can't make your own compost due to space constraints, living in a rented home, or being about to move. There are alternatives. Some local agencies and recycling centers offer free compost, made from collected garden and food waste, and others sell it for a small fee. The quantity and quality of available compost may vary, but it's well worth trying because it's usually produced on a large scale and heated so that most weed seeds are killed.

Mulches

A mulch is a layer of material to cover the soil around plants. Mulching saves time and money because it helps the soil retain moisture and suppresses weeds. A mulch of a natural material gradually mixes with the top layer of soil (helped by worms, which pull it down), improving soil structure. It keeps soil and roots cool in the summer and provides frost protection in the winter. It can also protect the soil from being washed away in heavy rain.

Natural materials suitable for mulching are mostly free and available from the house and garden. You can use grass cuttings (see below), wood or bark chippings, leaves, any brown or green shredded material from the garden, straw, well-rotted manure (from chickens and other farm animals), shredded recycled cardboard, and homemade compost. Wool sheets used for packaging also make an excellent mulch and are thought to deter slugs. Leaf mold is a mulch made of the decaying leaves of deciduous shrubs and trees.

Spring and fall are the best times to apply a mulch. Adding a layer of at least 2in (5cm) of mulch is perfect, and will really neaten up your borders, too.

Left Grass cuttings ready to spread around a plant as a mulch.

Grass cuttings

After cutting your grass, instead of putting the cuttings on the compost heap (though that's fine, too), you can place them as a mulch directly on borders or the vegetable patch. As worms pull the grass into the soil, it will be broken down, adding organic matter. The grass cuttings will release nutrients and improve soil structure as they act like a sponge, helping the soil retain moisture. An additional benefit is that as the earthworms burrow through the soil, they aerate it and provide drainage.

Before adding the grass as a mulch, make sure it has not been treated with fertilizer or weed killer, and that no flowers have set seeds.

....

Anya's top tip

Molehills are made up of fine, fluffy topsoil that can be mixed with potting mix and added to pots, especially larger ones where it would take a lot of mix to fill. It can also be added to improve the fertility of garden soil.

Fertilizing your soil the natural way

Making your own plant food is super easy and environmentally friendly, but also very cost-effective. And it really works! Nettles and comfrey are vigorous and leafy. You can cut them down to make free, nutritious fertilizer, and they rapidly regrow, so you can keep making more batches. Alternatively you can grow plants that act as a "green manure" to improve your soil.

Homemade fertilizers

Stinging nettles flourish in nitrogen-rich soil, which enables them to outcompete other plants. Their roots absorb the nitrogen from the soil, and the nitrogen is transferred into the leaves, which can then be used as a fertilizer. Nitrogen is particularly important for leafy growth, and perfect for feeding your plants in the spring when they are getting going after the winter. Nettles are also rich in iron, calcium, and magnesium. Comfrey leaves are rich in potassium, which is particularly important for flower and fruit production; I use it once plants have produced buds. They are great for feeding dahlias and other hungry plants. Comfrey is also full of nitrogen, phosphorus, vitamin B12, and many trace elements. If you water your plants once a week with the liquid fertilizer between April and October, you'll see a massive difference! Here I show you how to make a comfrey fertilizer, but the same method applies for nettles.

You will need

Pruners
Knife
Bucket of water

1. Harvest comfrey leaves, cutting them off the plant. Wear gloves to avoid the irritating hairs on the leaves and stems.

2. Gather enough leaves to fill a bucket.

3. Chop the leaves roughly.

4. Place the leaves in a bucket of water and cover with a lid (it will get smelly!). After 2–6 weeks the leaves will have rotted down and your feed is ready to use. Dilute at a rate of 1 part comfrey liquid to 10 parts water.

Green manure

These fast-growing plants are sown and then dug into the ground to add valuable nutrients and to improve soil structure, often in a vegetable bed between crops. The main aim is to add organic matter to the soil, but many also fix nitrogen (taking it from the air and adding it into the soil). In addition they suppress weeds by covering bare soil, and the flowering varieties are attractive to beneficial insects.

Some are grown from spring to fall, and others in fall and winter. Simply sow the seeds and rake them in. After 60–90 days, chop down the foliage and leave it to wilt for a few days on the soil surface. Dig the plants into the top 10in (25cm) of soil, then leave it for 2–3 weeks or more before cultivating.

Green manure plants suitable for fall sowing include *Phacelia tanacetifolia* (invasive in some regions); for spring and summer sowing try alsike clover (*Trifolium hybridum;* and in fall to winter sow ryegrass (*Lolium*) and white mustard (*Sinapis alba*).

1.

2.

3.

4.

Using water wisely, clockwise from top left: salvia is of Mediterranean origin, and so it's a good choice to withstand drought; poppies thrive in dry conditions; my rain barrel collects precious rainwater; watering selectively by hand, rather than using a sprinkler.

SAVING WATER

With the changing weather conditions, including extended droughts as well as more intensive rain, you need to make your garden more resilient to cope with extremes. There are quite a few measures that you can build in to help your garden thrive while minimizing water use.

Using water efficiently in the garden helps the environment and saves you time and money—it makes sense on all fronts.

Collecting water

Rain barrels are a useful part of your garden infrastructure. Located under a downspout on a house or a gutter on a shed or outbuilding, a rain barrel will collect rainwater ready for you to use during dry spells. You can also collect household wastewater from washing dishes, the bath, or when cleaning a fish tank. Make sure the water doesn't contain any chemicals, and only very minimal dirt or detergent, before using it to water plants. If I wash down things such as pots in the garden, I always wash them over a border, or collect the water in a plastic trug or wheelbarrow so that it can be reused.

Using water carefully

Water is a precious resource, so it needs to be used carefully to best effect. I always water newly planted plants until they are established, and make sure my cuttings don't dry out. I never water grass; even if it is parched in the summer, it will green up again. Watering in the morning or evening minimizes evaporation from both plants and soil, so the watering has the maximum benefit. Mulching (see pp.68–69) reduces evaporation immediately around a plant's roots, so is well worth doing. I also line terracotta pots and hanging baskets with plastic potting mix bags cut to size (but with drainage holes). This reduces evaporation through the sides of the container.

If you are using a hose for watering, check it for leaks and replace linking parts as needed. Avoid using sprinklers in the garden; they water a huge area instead of targeting the plants that need water, so they are not efficient.

Adapting your planting

If conditions in your garden are changing so that it regularly dries out for prolonged periods, it's worth consciously choosing and planting more drought-tolerant plants. These will thrive in the drier conditions, and save money because you will not need to water them so much. You will be enabling your garden to adapt to the new conditions.

Drought-tolerant perennials include agapanthus, lady's mantle (*Alchemilla mollis*), crocosmia, various poppies (*Papaver*), and catmint (*Nepeta*). For shrubs, choose lavender, buddleia, santolina, cotoneaster, and eleagnus. Many herbs, such as bay, dill, sage, thyme, and rosemary flourish and have a more intense flavor in dry conditions. There are many more plants that will tolerate dry conditions, and these are very useful in containers as well as in the wider garden.

KEEPING PLANTS HEALTHY

Many so-called "pests" or diseases are part of our garden's ecosystem, and every little element of the ecosystem is there for a reason. Using chemicals and pesticides to remove one element might have damaging consequences that will cost money. In many cases even pests can be seen as useful friends, making gardening more affordable.

For garden ailments, prevention is better than cure. Providing optimal conditions for plants (see p.18), following organic principles such as ensuring the soil is healthy, and truly understanding how the ecosystem works are the keys to keeping your garden in good health. This can help to ensure "pests" don't get out of control. Equally, diseases in the garden aren't welcome, but there are steps you can take to reduce the risk of them.

Choosing plants carefully

In addition to choosing plants that are suited to your garden in terms of aspect, soil, and climate (see p.16), you can also choose strong varieties that are more resistant to pests and diseases. A lot of useful information is found on plant labels and packets of seeds or by simply checking online. The All-America Selections (AAS, see p.80) is a great indicator of what to go for as many are chosen for the AAS because they have proved to be resistant to certain diseases. As soon as you find a plant that does well, propagate it and repeat it around the garden.

Dealing with damage

Healthy plants can withstand some insect activity. The damage a few snails or caterpillars will make may be almost unnoticeable if the plant is large and thriving, and if there are natural predators around. Slugs and snails are eaten by frogs, toads, centipedes, ground beetles, slow worms, and some birds. Caterpillars are essential for several bird species to gather as food for their young. All the beneficial predator species need to be encouraged in your garden. Often considered a nuisance, wasps are in fact the gardener's friend. They have the ability to communicate to other members of the colony about the best food sources, so they can methodically remove caterpillars that have built up on a crop.

There are a few things you can do if you see your plants being damaged. It's always worth inspecting your plants regularly so that you can sort out any problems—and check attack-prone plants such as hostas or dahlias as often as you can. I pick off some insects, slugs, and snails. Simply moving them away from their target plant (perhaps onto the compost heap) can give the plant some time to recover. I wash off some insects with water too—such as aphids off roses. They drop to the floor and it interrupts their feeding.

Friend and foe, clockwise from top left: a garden snail waiting for the thrush to find it; the caterpillar of a mullein moth feeding on *Verbascum chaixii*; blackfly on a dogwood (*Cornus*) shoot; a honeybee feeding on the nectar-rich flowers of the green manure *Phacelia tanacetifolia* (invasive in some regions).

CHAPTER 4
KNOW BEFORE YOU GROW

Although sometimes you might fall in love
with a plant, it's best to understand a bit
more about its needs and how it grows before
spending money on it. You can then ensure
you're choosing something that will thrive
in your garden and be a good value
in every sense.

UNDERSTANDING PLANTS

Knowing how different types of plants grow helps you plan your garden and to choose plants that are the best value for your budget—as well as making your garden look fabulous.

Gardening isn't about randomly buying plants that look good in their flowering season. Although sometimes you might fall in love with a plant, it's best to understand a bit more about its needs and how it grows before parting with your money so that you can ensure you're choosing something that will thrive in your garden and be a good value.

Not all plants have the same lifespan. There are three main groups, defined by how long they live: perennials, annuals, and biennials.

Perennials

Perennial plants will live for more than two years and may live for many. This large group of plants includes shrubs and trees, which have a woody structure that grows and lasts. Shrubs tend to have multiple woody stems, while trees usually have a single trunk. Trees and shrubs can be evergreen or deciduous (losing their leaves in winter to conserve energy).

"Herbaceous" perennials push their fresh, new stems above ground in spring, bloom over spring and summer, then die back in fall and winter, returning with new growth the following spring. Ornamental grasses can be annual or perennial.

Left This summery mixture includes the perennials astrantia and geranium, with the deep red biennial rose campion (*Lychnis*).

Climbers are plants that make long stems which scramble up and over a supporting structure; they can be annuals, biennials, or perennials, including shrubs.

Bulbs are perennials that die back each year, storing their energy underground, ready to grow strongly the following spring. The term "bulb" is often used to cover all sorts of underground storage parts, including corms, rhizomes, and tubers. These are all formed from modified plant parts: a bulb (such as a daffodil) is made up of layers of leaves; a corm (such as crocosmia) is a swollen, rounded underground stem; a rhizome (such as an iris) is also an underground stem; and tubers (such as dahlias) can be underground stems or roots. I'm using "bulb" to cover all of these plants.

Annuals and biennials

As their name suggests, annuals are plants that live for only one year. Their life cycle from germination to the production of seeds will be completed within one growing season, and then they die. Their seeds will germinate the following growing season to restart the cycle.

Biennials live for two years, growing leaves in their first year and flowering the following year. Some plants that are usually biennial can live longer, depending on the weather and growing conditions. They might surprise you with an additional few years.

SPENDING WELL

Although there are many ways to obtain plants for free, especially by propagating them (see pp.110–59), sometimes you need to buy plants—perhaps when you are starting out, or if you want a particular variety, or to fill a space quickly. It makes sense to get the best value for your money instead of giving in to impulse. A little planning can help you spend well.

A basic rule of thumb for buying plants is that annuals and biennials are cheaper, especially if grown from seed or from tiny "plug" plants, while perennials are more expensive. It's more complicated than that, though. Buying annual or biennial "bedding" plants ready to flower is pricey—you will get an almost instant display of flowers, but then the plants will die. Although perennials, and especially shrubs and trees, are more of an investment, they will form the structure of your garden and come back year after year, making them better value, long-lasting, and low maintenance.

Making savings

One of the things I have learned over the years is that if you provide the right conditions, most plants will grow faster than you think. This means that buying them as seedlings often pays off, or, in the case of trees, you can buy them as saplings, and they will soon settle in and catch up in size to a more expensive, mature tree. Quite a few perennial plants, such as roses, peonies, and trees, can be purchased as bare-rooted plants (see p.83). These are cheaper than pot-grown plants but grow just as well.

If there's a plant you really like, check how easy it is to propagate. If you can't find one to propagate for free, from a friend or neighbor's garden, you could buy one plant and make many more from it.

It's a good idea to visit gardens and garden centers every month of the year, not necessarily to buy, but to see what's in season and what's in flower, taking notes and researching your plants to see if they suit the conditions and space available in your garden. When you see a special offer, if one of the plants on your wish list is among them, that's a good time to buy. The clearance section of a garden center is always worth checking out, but especially in the fall (see p.177). Even if plants don't look like anything special, if you look after them they will often return to their former glory.

Anya's top tip

One indicator of a great-value plant is the All-America Selections (AAS) Winner award. You might have seen the logo on labels and in plant descriptions. This is awarded by the independent AAS nonprofit after testing for superior garden performance by horticulture professionals across North America. The AAS Winner award gives you peace of mind that your money is well spent.

Plants offering excellent value, clockwise from top left: *Cotinus coggygria* 'Royal Purple' establishes well from semiripe cuttings; *Dahlia* 'Night Silence' is one of many dahlias that reproduce easily from basal cuttings or by dividing the tubers; chives are simple to divide; this giant blue hosta (*H. sieboldiana* var. *elegans*) was bought as a tiny plant and is now a large clump that can be divided.

SHRUBS AND TREES

These woody stalwarts are the backbone of the garden, giving it shape and interest all year round, offering height, a green backdrop, and often stunning flowers and sometimes berries. They can be grouped or grown as a hedge, or planted on their own as a feature. If you buy and plant them carefully, they will reward you for many years.

For a major long-term purchase such as a tree or shrub—sometimes major in terms of cost, always in terms of its place in your garden—research is your friend.

Choosing a tree

There's a tree for every garden, large or small, but choosing the right one can be a challenge. Think of its ultimate size. Time flies, and what was a lovely little tree can turn into a large one, taking over half of your garden.

In addition to height, consider features such as bark texture, overall shape, whether the tree is evergreen, and flower color and timing. Think about the leaves. Dense trees may create unwanted shade (like some magnolias, which have fabulous spring flowers but large leaves), while others such as birch have smaller, sparser leaves, creating dappled shade. Trees that produce berries or fruit are lovely to look at and attract birds that will eat slugs and snails.

Having a larger garden will give you more options—you can think big and plant an orchard or small glade of trees. But there are so many wonderful trees for small spaces, too. Ornamental cherries (such as the winter-flowering *Prunus* x *subhirtella* 'Autumnalis

Rosea'), Japanese maples (*Acer*), and eastern redbuds (*Cercis canadensis*) all offer multiple features and fit well in a smaller garden.

Choosing a shrub

Shrubs are low maintenance but maximum impact. Two favorites are Japanese snowball (*Viburnum plicatum* f. *tomentosum* 'Mariesii'), with its breathtakingly large white late spring flowers, and the evergreen *Hebe* 'Midsummer Beauty', which offers something all year. Most shrubs are easy to propagate by cuttings (see pp.114–35) or layering (see pp.144–47), so you can quickly create more.

When to buy

Many trees and shrubs are available bare-rooted when they are dormant in fall and winter. These are always much cheaper than those in pots. Don't be discouraged by the smaller size—they will take slightly longer to get established, but after three or four years will put on significant growth. Hedging plants are best to buy bare-rooted, and in late winter they are often reduced in price.

You can buy plants in pots all year. The ideal plant has healthy top growth and roots that are developed but not overcrowded. But I have bought some hopeless-looking specimens for a great price that have made great mature plants with good aftercare.

Left A deep purple twisted hazel tree (*Corylus avellana* 'Red Majestic') stands out against *Cotinus coggygria* 'Young Lady' in flower.

Caring for shrubs and trees

The best time for planting bare-root trees and shrubs is between fall and spring, but avoid frosty days and waterlogged ground. They should be planted as soon as you can after buying. If you need to delay, place them in a bucket filled with potting mix and keep them for a few days in a shady, frost-free place such as your shed or garage until they can go in the ground. If you buy trees or shrubs grown in containers, they can be planted any time of the year following the same method as with bare-rooted plants, but avoid extreme conditions such as heat or frost. If you can't plant them for quite a while, repot them into a bigger pot so that they have enough space.

Before planting, always inspect your tree or shrub and remove any stems or roots that look shriveled or damaged. Dig a hole and place the plant in it to check planting depth. You want it to be at the level of the planting mark on the bark of a bare-root plant (this is the line visible on the bark showing where the soil reached when it was previously planted), or at the same level as the top of the soil in the container. Make sure that the hole is big enough for the roots to spread, then cover them with soil, firming as you go.

Stake trees well so that the roots establish and are not displaced by strong winds. Secure the tree to the stake with a thick tree tie to avoid damaging the bark, and check it regularly, loosening it as the tree grows.

After planting, your new tree or shrub will need to be watered well. Keep checking and watering regularly in the first 12 months, especially during dry spells, and never let the ground dry out completely. Add a mulch (see p.69) in the spring to help suppress weeds, removing any that develop around the tree.

If you are unsure of what to do at any stage of planting or growing your new tree, check the Arbor Day Foundation's website for extra advice (arborday.org/trees/tips/). Pruning is something that some trees and shrubs really benefit from as they become established, although others can be left alone. Again, the Arbor Day Foundation website has guidance about timing and how to prune.

Moving a tree

If a tree or shrub is in the wrong place, rather than cutting it down or buying another for a different part of the garden, it's possible to move it with great care—as long as it's not too large to lift. You need to cut the roots off up to 20in (50cm) away from the trunk (depending on the size of the plant), and leave it like that for about six months. As you lift the plant during the dormant season, cut the roots growing down into the ground, then move it in a wheelbarrow to its new place. Water in dry spells for about a year until it has established.

Right If you have moved a tree, check for leaf buds the following spring as a sign that the tree has responded well to the change.

PERENNIALS

Perennial plants are your wallet's best friend. They really save money, offering low cost and a large impact. Not only do most perennial plants last for many years, but lots of them can grow in pots and containers, as well as in garden borders.

The range of perennials to choose from is incredible and slightly bewildering. Some like shade (like hellebores), others sun (such as lavender). There are perennials that live for decades, and others that last only a few years. By planting them in the right place and providing the right conditions, you can get the most for your money: they'll grow rapidly and can be easily propagated.

Choosing perennial plants

Think about what you want from your perennials. Narrow down your options by considering a few factors. First, look at the season of interest: how long is it? Do you need a plant to offer its best at a certain time? Then consider conditions in your garden: do you need a plant to screen a fence, for shade, or for very dry soil, or for acid soil, or for a pot? These needs will all rule out certain plants and focus your search. What size plant do you need for the space you have available? Look at the final size of the plant, and think about whether this will work in the space you have. Finally, is the plant an AAS Winner (see p.80)? If so, you can have confidence that you are getting good value.

Left For a late summer and early fall display, *Dahlia* 'Ken's Rarity' and aster (*Symphyotrichum novi-belgii* 'White Ladies') keep flowering until the first frost.

Perhaps you want to make a fabulous display of pots? With its neat habit and colorful, succulent leaves, *Sempervivum* is perfect for outdoor planters. Agapanthus will perform best when its roots are restricted, and if you're growing it in a container it's easy to care for and should need repotting only every five to seven years.

Grasses are an overlooked perennial plant and well worth considering. They add texture and movement, and sometimes when planted in the right place where they catch the sun, they can look truly magical. Grasses are wonderful for mixing with other plants, and many grasses can be grown in pots. My favorite ornamental grass is Lessing feather grass (*Stipa lessingiana*). I grow it in pots as a single plant, but it also looks amazing when planted with other perennials such as gauras, Mexican daisy (*Erigeron karvinskianus*), or dahlias.

Caring for perennials

For me, plants are like members of my family, and I look after them accordingly. Some don't need much attention, but most perennial plants benefit from some extra care and understanding of their needs. When you add new perennial plants to your garden, make sure the surrounding soil is weed-free. Prepare the soil by adding lots of well-rotted manure.

By feeding, mulching, watering, cutting back, and supporting (see pp.48–49), you will get more from your plants. Feeding your plants, in most cases, will ensure that they perform all summer, but remember that there are also some, such as lavender, that prefer poor soil, and they don't need to be given any extra fertilizers. As a general guideline for hungrier plants, you can add a slow-release fertilizer such as bone meal or chicken pellets in the early spring. Most plants benefit from extra potassium or nitrogen given when they actively grow. You can make your own natural fertilizers using stinging nettles or comfrey (see pp.70–71).

It's your choice whether you cut back herbaceous perennials when they die back in the fall or just as new growth is starting in spring, but leaving them until spring is more wildlife friendly because you will create shelter and provide food to an enormous amount of wildlife. That wildlife will pay you back by making your garden pest-free. Win-win, and such a cost-effective option.

It's worth checking more individual care needs too. Lavender, for example, needs particular pruning to stay healthy: French lavender (*Lavandula stoechas*) has to be deadheaded in the summer, gently trimmed at the end of the season after flowering, and trimmed again in April. Other lavenders benefit from pruning at different times.

After two to five years, most perennial plants will benefit from division (see pp.136–41). Lifting and dividing will not only rejuvenate your perennials, but it'll also create more plants for free (see below).

I would recommend consulting your local extension office about pruning and feeding and all the extra care that will make your plants shine, tailoring your approach to each species. Letting things be can sometimes be just what is needed.

Perennials for free

The joy of perennials is how easy they are to propagate. If you're starting from scratch, you may be able to obtain seeds, cuttings, and mini plants from friends to get you started. Once you have a few perennial plants, you can use them to create many more. A lot of perennial plants such as verbascums, Mexican daisy, campanulas, and more will gently self-seed, which saves not only money but also time. Every year I let my mature hellebore plants create more seedlings and move them to where I want around the garden (see p.17).

Many plants simply look better when planted in groups, as hedges, or even en masse. It becomes more affordable to do this with cuttings (see pp.114–35). *Hydrangea arborescens* 'Annabelle' (see pp.90–91) and *H. paniculata* 'Limelight' are my favorites, and they look lovely as single plants—but as a hedge? Wow! Hydrangeas are so easy to propagate by taking cuttings; within two or three years you will have hundreds of plants identical to the parent plant.

And I've already mentioned division, which is necessary to keep perennials healthy but also enables you to create hundreds of new plants that will be immediately garden ready. Unlike cuttings or seeds, division gives you an instant-impact result.

Herbaceous perennials, clockwise from top left: *Euphorbia characias* subsp. *wulfenii* offers a fantastic early spring display in full sun, and it self-seeds; aquilegia self-seeds and flourishes in sun and partial shade; lady's mantle (*Alchemilla mollis*) is an iconic cottage garden plant, very easy to grow and reproduce from seed or division; *Astrantia major* is easily divided in spring or fall.

Overleaf A hedge of *Hydrangea arborescens* 'Annabelle' in flower.

ANNUALS AND BIENNIALS

Growing annuals and biennials can be a great money saver, because they can all be grown from seed, which is always a more cost-effective option. What could save you even more is the fact that you can easily collect your own seeds from your garden.

Annuals and biennials mature quickly and will add color and texture within a few months after sowing. You can fill a new border or garden with them until the perennial plants mature. This makes them ideal for renters who don't know how long they'll be in a garden, but who want to have some color and variety. Almost all of them are fabulous in containers too, which can be moved to a more prominent position when the plants are looking their best. If you grow a variety and enjoy it, you can collect the seeds (see pp.148–51) or buy new ones and start the cycle again.

Annuals have so much to offer. Many are garden staples every summer with their huge variety of flowers of all shapes and sizes. Love-in-a-mist (*Nigella damascena*) is one of my particular favorites. Its delicate foliage and flowers will soften the edges of paths, adding texture and color, and its flowers can be used for arrangements, both fresh and dry. It doesn't like to be transplanted, and that's why you'll never see it sold in pots. Cosmos is another must-have plant. It gives you masses of flowers, blooming for months from early summer until

the first frost. It's perfect for cut flowers: the blooms last long in a vase. It's also loved by bees, butterflies, moths, and other pollinators.

Biennial plants often self-seed regularly. So while they are flowering, the seedlings from the previous year are growing, ready to provide color the following summer. My favorite biennials are foxgloves (*Digitalis*), and honesty (*Lunaria annua*). All produce lots of seeds to collect, and they self-seed around the garden. For more about how to identify and transplant self-sown seedlings, see pp.94–95.

Sowing annuals and biennials

If the seeds are sown at the right time, you'll have nature on your side and you don't need any propagators or other expensive equipment. A seed packet always tells you when to sow, but otherwise check to get the timing right. Many seedlings will be frost tender, so if you sow in colder months, protect your precious young plants until the frosts have passed.

For how to sow seeds, see pp.152–57. It may be tempting to sow more than you need, but think of what you can use in your garden; imagine how many plants you would buy at a garden center and add a few more. If you do end up with too many, pass them on to family and friends or a plant sale.

Left Tall, white *Verbascum chaixii* 'Wedding Candles' contrasts with the vivid biennial rose campion (*Lychnis*).

Anya's top tip

Sow seeds of love-in-a-mist (*Nigella damascena*) every four weeks from late spring to early summer for a continuous succession of blooms.

Pinching out

If you're growing your annuals and biennials from seed, taking care of your seedlings in the early stages is key. Their natural growth habit is to put their energy into developing tall stems. If you leave them to their own devices, this will result in "leggy" plants that have a tendency to flop over and produce fewer flowers. Pinching out is a very simple type of pruning where the growing tip of a main stem is removed. This encourages plants to make new side shoots along the stem so that the whole plant becomes fuller and bushier, and it will produce more flowers. In most cases I pinch out seedlings as soon as they have developed two sets of true leaves—these are the leaves that look like the leaves of the adult plant, rather than the simpler ones that grow first from the seed. After pinching out, I transplant my seedlings into their individual pots (see pp.154–57).

Annuals and biennials that need to be pinched out include petunias, cosmos, sweet peas (*Lathyrus odoratus*), snapdragons (*Antirrhinum*), marigolds (*Tagetes* and *Calendula*), busy lizzies (*Impatiens*), and cerinthe. Avoid pinching out sunflowers (*Helianthus annuus*).

Self-sown seedlings

If you want to make the most of self-sown seedlings, you need to be able to tell them apart from weed seedlings so that you don't pull them out by mistake. Some look like tiny versions of the parent plant, while others change as they mature. Foxgloves, for example, start with round leaves and then the leaves become oval. You can easily look up images of different stages of plant development if you're not sure, and after a while you'll know exactly what you are looking for.

If the seedlings are in the right place, let them be; if not, they can be transplanted carefully to the most suitable place in your garden. Many seedlings in borders will benefit from being moved so they are not overshadowed by fast-growing, mature plants. Transplant them with some moist soil around their roots.

A lot of seedlings such as foxgloves (*Digitalis*), rose campion (*Lychnis coronaria*), and verbascum can be easily transplanted. Others such as honesty (*Lunaria annua*) and opium poppies don't like to be transplanted, so you just need to let them grow where they are.

Deadheading

Most annuals and biennials benefit from deadheading—the removal of flowers from plants when they start to fade. As soon as the flowers fade, plants start creating seeds, using a lot of energy to do so. If you remove the fading flowers by pinching or cutting them off, the plant will instead create more flowers for us to enjoy and for insects to feed on. Regular deadheading directs energy into stronger growth and more flowers over a longer period. If you want to save seeds from a plant (see pp.148–51), stop deadheading when the weather starts to cool down to allow the seeds time to ripen.

Easy annuals and biennials from seed, clockwise from top left: self-sown foxglove (*Digitalis*) seedlings can be left to grow, or transplanted; rose campion (*Lychnis*) is another biennial that self seeds freely; love-in-a-mist (*Nigellla damascena*) does not need deadheading because its seed pods are attractive; cosmos are tender, so they need to be sown indoors and transplanted outside.

CLIMBERS

Don't neglect the vertical surfaces in your garden. Climbers can be used for screening and to provide privacy, as well as on freestanding supports to give height in borders and in containers. They are really useful in small spaces, offering flowers and scent, fall colors, berries, and interesting textures.

Climbers grow up a vertical surface using tendrils or stems that twine. Some, such as ivy, have roots growing from the stem that stick to walls. Others may need to be tied in to a support. They can be shrubs, perennials, or annuals, and may be evergreen or deciduous.

Choosing a climber

First look for climbers to suit the site in terms of aspect and soil (you can always improve the soil for a long-term climber, see pp.66–69), then narrow down to find one that provides the color and level of density that you want. Evergreen climbers offer privacy and cover an unsightly surface. Lighter climbers, such as some clematis or annuals, might be more suitable on a freestanding support or in a container. Always check on the vigor, too—there's nothing worse than constantly having to cut back a vigorous climber. Some climbers such as wisteria are very strong and can block pipes and gutters, or damage the surface of the walls. But vigorous climbers, including some roses, may be perfect to climb into an old tree or cover a large garden wall.

Climbers usually need support via a trellis, wires fixed to a wall or fence, or a freestanding structure. Even self-clinging climbers need a few canes or a small trellis to start them off. You can create your own supports to save expense (see pp.48–49, 166–69).

Many climbers are easy to propagate, so before you spend any money, see whether any of your friends or neighbors have the plant you like. It's simple to layer a stem of a climbing hydrangea or wisteria (see pp.144–47), so kindly asking and creating your own plants for free is the way forward.

Annual climbers are a short-term solution for a burst of color or if you're renting or moving soon, or to provide color while you're propagating perennial climbers. Grow annual climbers from seed, and they will flower the same year. I recommend sweet peas (*Lathyrus odoratus*), morning glory (*Ipomoea*), cup-and-saucer vine (*Cobaea scandens*), and black-eyed Susan (*Thunbergia alata* 'African Sunset').

For longer-term climbers in sun, choose from wisteria, climbing roses (most like full sun), jasmine (*Jasminum officinale*), clematis, and passionflower (*Passiflora*). For light shade try *Hydrangea petiolaris*, *Schizophragma hydrangeoides*, some ivies (*Hedera*), and clematis 'Jackmanii'. The climbing roses 'Madame Alfred Carrière' and 'New Dawn' will grow in light shade. For full shade, ivies and Virginia creepers (including *Parthenocissus henryana* and *P. quinquefolia*) offer beautiful foliage.

Right The tender annual *Ipomoea* 'Star of Yelta' is supported by a trellis on a brick wall.

BULBS

An easy way to add interest and color to any garden, bulbs are like floral fireworks. There are bulbs for any style or taste, from cottage to contemporary, and varieties that flower from late winter to fall. They're also a low-maintenance option. Here I'm using the word "bulbs" to include flowers that grow from corms, rhizomes, and tubers (see p.79), as well as from true bulbs.

Incredibly versatile in the garden, some bulbs grow very well when naturalized in grass, as well as in your borders. Most can be planted in pots (on their own or mixed with other plants), which means that they can be grown in the smallest garden or even on a balcony or windowsill. They generally prefer sun or at least a good level of light to thrive, but some, such as snowdrops, will tolerate slight shade.

Choosing bulbs

To get the most for your money, do your research to make sure your bulbs will be productive for years to come. Bulbs such as spring daffodils, snowdrops, and crocuses, or summer alliums and lilies are really productive and flower reliably year after year. Many tulips perform well for only one season, and they aren't cheap, so think carefully before you buy. There are some good perennial tulips (such as 'Groenland', 'Spring Green', 'Artist', Shirley', 'Negrita', and 'Apeldoorn') that will naturalize, so if you really love tulips, choose these instead of the annual varieties (see also pp.178–79). Read the description to make sure you're buying the right kind.

Left This pale cream double daffodil (*Narcissus* 'White Lion') naturalizes well in grass.

The most cost-effective way of introducing bulbs to your garden is by purchasing them in the fall. If you buy in bulk, you will save on cost. A few types are available as potted bulbs in the springtime, known as "in the green." These are expensive, but if you buy them reduced at the end of the season, they will come up again the following season.

Before buying, check the flowering time so that you can plan a succession of blooms. If you plan wisely, just the bulbs themselves will give you flowers for months. One of the best birthday gifts I have received was thousands of daffodil bulbs from my mother-in-law. She said she wanted me to have fresh flowers for months and together we chose the varieties, making sure they would flower in waves. Planting them among trees has created so much interest and my thousands of daffodils are a spring highlight. They have filled a large area of our garden, making it low maintenance.

There are so many alliums to choose from for summer impact in your garden. For the more expensive varieties, plant a small group and gradually add to your collection. *Allium hollandicum* 'Purple Sensation' is more cost effective and can be planted en masse in your borders among herbaceous perennials and ornamental grasses, or in wildflower meadows where its leaves will be hidden as they die back.

Anya's top tip

Create a list of bulbs you like that you want to add to your garden. Each year check whether any are available discounted (usually half price) in late winter. This way you can gradually fill your garden with bulbs for a fraction of the price. Many bulbs, especially tulips, can be planted even during the winter months, which means that even if you buy your bulbs much later, you can still plant them in the garden or in pots, but you'll spend less.

Planting bulbs

In general, bulbs need to be planted at a depth that is three times the height of the bulb—but check each type for specific requirements. Daffodils, crocuses, snowdrops, and other spring-flowering types need to be planted in the fall. Tulips need to be planted later in the fall or even early winter. Tender summer bulbs such as gladioli should be planted in spring, and fall-flowering nerines between spring and summer. Don't worry too much if you are slightly late. Life can get in the way, and I have planted daffodils in late February just because I didn't get a chance to do it in the fall. I'm not saying it's the best thing to do, but I know from my own experience that bulbs can be very forgiving, and the ones I planted in February did very well.

Although snowdrops and muscari can be grown in the ground, they also make great plants in pots, flowering at a time when there is little other color in the garden. Placed on the garden table they will be perfectly displayed, and will come back each year. Both are easy to divide into more plants (see pp.140–41).

Caring for bulbs

Most bulbs are pretty self-sufficient. Once planted, they don't require much attention. That's why they are such a great addition to any garden. Sometimes mice or squirrels can dig up bulbs in pots; if they're a problem, cover your pot with chicken wire until the bulbs come up.

After they have finished flowering, bulbs need to gather much-needed energy to perform the following year. They gather that energy through their foliage and take it back down to the bulb to store. It's therefore very important to let the foliage die back naturally. Just think of the foliage as charging the batteries; let your bulbs be charged after such a performance. If you have grown bulbs in pots, you could move them into the ground to die down because they will receive more nutrients than in a pot.

Tender, summer-flowering bulbs, such as dahlias, need to be lifted and stored over winter to plant outside again the following late spring. Keep dahlia tubers in a dry, dark place, with potting mix around them, to prevent them from rotting. If you want to lift other bulbs, dry them out and keep them in the dark (in a labeled paper bag if possible) until it's time to plant them. Remember that mice love bulbs (because they are so full of nutritious energy); and if you store them somewhere outside, there's a chance mice will feast on them.

Right I grow muscari for cheerful pot displays in spring. On the left is *Muscari aucheri* 'Ocean Magic', with *M.* 'Baby's Breath' on the right.

A FEW FAVORITES

These plants are some of the favorites in my garden, ones that I find offer amazing value for money as well as value in terms of being beautiful, versatile, and resilient. I've included a range for many situations and uses. I hope you enjoy trying out some of them in your garden.

NETTLE-LEAVED MULLEIN
Verbascum chaixii
'Wedding Candles'

This perennial plant has a rosette of leaves at the base from which the tall flower spikes (up to about 3ft/1m) rise all summer. It gently self-seeds, producing hundreds of new plants in one season. Loved by pollinators, it's easy and rewarding to grow.

AMERICAN ASTER
Symphyotrichum

These late summer and fall-flowering herbaceous perennials provide valuable food for pollinators in late summer, when other sources are fading. With their cheerful, daisylike flowers, mostly in shades of pink, blue, purple, and white, they combine well with other perennials such as dahlias. They range in height and density from delicate sprays of blooms to vivid, eye-catching clumps. You can propagate them by softwood cuttings (see pp.122–25) and division (see pp.137–39).

YARROW
Achillea

Another huge group of herbaceous perennials, yarrows are very easy to grow from seed, and produce flowers in their first year. The structural, flat flower heads come in colors from yellow and orange to pink and white. My favorites are 'Pearl, 'Love Parade', and all the pastel shades. They reach about 3ft (1m), depending on the variety. Pollinators love them, and they make fantastic cut flowers. You can collect and save the seeds to sow (see pp.148–55).

GARDEN PHLOX
Phlox paniculata

This highly scented perennial is available in many shades of pink, purple, white, and orange. It adds interest in mid- to late summer, reaching up to 5ft (1.5m), depending on the variety; some are much smaller. It's easy to propagate by division in spring or fall (see pp.137–39), by softwood or basal cuttings in spring (see pp.122–25), semi-ripe cuttings in late summer (see pp.126–29), or even root cuttings in fall and winter. (see p.133).

LONDON PRIDE
Saxifraga x *urbium*

This evergreen perennial makes wonderful and very attractive ground cover, and looks beautiful when planted en masse at the front of a sunny border. With its frothy, pinky white flowers, borne above the leaves in summer, it reaches about 12in (30cm) tall. It's very easy to propagate by detaching rosettes and rooting them after flowering in late spring to mid-summer (see pp.138–39).

PAINTED SAGE
Salvia viridis

This annual plant is mainly grown for its "flowers," which are in fact colorful modified leaves (bracts). It makes a great cut flower, but I also add it to my borders as a filler. It is fast growing (up to about 12in/30cm), and easy to grow from seed. I love the fact that this plant self-seeds gently, giving me seedlings for free without me having to use trays. Seedlings can be collected in early spring and transplanted to where you want—it likes a sunny spot, but grows in a variety of soils.

STRAWFLOWER
Xerochrysum bracteatum

I love strawflowers for their dual purpose as fresh and dried flowers. I not only grow them in my cutting garden, but also add them to my borders to fill the gaps. These annuals are easy to grow from seed (see pp.152–55), and can also be propagated by using the pinched-out tips of the stems (see pp.122–25) to create more plants that will flower slightly later in the season, providing more flowers at the end of the summer.

SMOKE TREE
Cotinus coggygria

Smoke tree is one of my favorite shrubs because of its long season of interest. It has deep red leaves from spring, turning beautiful shades in fall. The tiny summer flowers grow in plumes that give the plant its name. There are many varieties available in various colors and sizes; it can grow to up to 26ft (8m) tall and wide. It's easy to propagate by air layering (see p.147).

ALLIUM
Allium hollandicum
'Purple Sensation'

Probably one of my favorite of all spring-flowering bulbs. This very striking allium has round purple flowerheads of star-shaped flowers that last for a few weeks and make great cut flowers and dry well. It's not as expensive as some other varieties and great to plant en masse in a meadow or a border. It can reach 3ft (90cm) tall. If the leaves are visible in a border, aim to have other plants growing up through them or in front of them to disguise them as they die back.

FORGET-ME-NOT
(SCORPION GRASSES)
Myosotis

Flowering in spring for several weeks in spring, forget-me-nots are lovely in containers or planted with tulips. Although they have a reputation of being slightly invasive, I find these annuals a useful addition for money-saving gardeners because their seedlings can be moved and planted in pots to save money on expensive bedding plants. If you have too many, the seedlings are easy to pull out and give away or put on the compost heap.

FOAMFLOWER
Tiarella 'Spring Symphony'

This is a new plant for me. I only discovered this small, pretty herbaceous perennial in the past few years, but I love to grow it in pots and in the garden. It's a wonderful addition to a shady spot. The leaves have purple along the ribs, and it bears pale pink flowers in spring, growing to about 12in (30cm) tall. Plants can be divided in spring (see pp.138–39).

SWEET ROCKET (DAME'S ROCKET)
Hesperis matronalis

One of my favorite biennial plants, sweet rocket is in some cases a short-lived perennial. It has fragrant white or purple flowers in clusters in late spring to early summer, sometimes reaching 3ft (90cm). It is easily grown by sowing seeds in trays in early spring (see pp.152–55) or direct sowing in midsummer (see pp.156–57). Ripe seeds can be collected in the garden and used for sowing in the future (see pp.148–51). Considered invasive in some regions.

CHAPTER 5

PLANTS FOR FREE

Growing plants from scratch, making use of their natural ways of reproducing, is a fascinating and rewarding process. The best part is that anyone can do it, making dreamy gardens achievable at a fraction of the cost of buying plants.

WHAT IS PROPAGATION?

Put simply, propagation means that you reproduce plants yourself. It's a great way to save money because it enables you to increase your stock at very little or no expense—just a handful of seeds or cuttings can produce a border packed with plants. Once you've mastered a few surprisingly simple techniques, a little really can go a long way.

Propagation may sound complicated and a bit daunting, but it's essentially a natural process that occurs in our gardens all the time.

Learning from nature

Plants have evolved many natural ways to reproduce: some from seeds dispersed by wind, animals, or water and transported to a new site where they germinate and produce new plants; others from bits of stem that have broken off or spread along the soil and formed new roots. Clumps of plants may also be divided into pieces, perhaps by an animal digging or water eroding the soil. If there is enough root intact, each piece can grow to form a new plant. This is how plants colonize new areas.

As gardeners, we replicate these natural reproductive techniques when we sow seeds, take cuttings, divide clumps of perennials, and layer shrubs or climbers. Growing plants from scratch is a fascinating and rewarding process, and the best part is that anyone can do it, making dreamy gardens achievable at a fraction of the cost of buying plants.

Left Some plants look better en masse, but this is expensive to do if you have to buy them all. Propagation allows you to create hundreds of plants for free.

The cost-saving benefits

In all cases, it's much cheaper or even free to propagate your own plants—perhaps sourcing the original plant from a friend, family member, neighbor, or community garden—than to buy established plants at high individual cost from a garden center or nursery.

Propagation is particularly beneficial if you want to include multiples of the same plant in the garden. Many perennials—such as black-eyed Susan (*Rudbeckia*), heucheras, echinaceas, and asters (*Symphyotrichum novi-belgii*)—look better planted in groups or drifts, and you can create a beautiful hedge by planting a row of the same type of tree or shrub, including cottage-garden favorites such as lavender, hydrangeas, and roses. Mimicking self-seeding annuals by sprinkling handfuls of saved seeds around borders or pots also looks attractive and fills space quickly, reducing the need to go and buy more plants.

Understanding a little about propagation also promotes self-sufficiency, and plant- or seed-swapping with other gardeners reduces waste. It can also quickly become addictive, as you see ever more opportunities to propagate plants from your collection, or seek out cuttings or seeds elsewhere.

PROPAGATION TYPES AND TIMINGS

In order to understand how to propagate plants in the garden, it helps to know how and when they reproduce in the wild. Following a few simple guidelines and providing the most favorable conditions certainly increases your chance of success, but don't be afraid of a bit of trial and error. Some of the best gardens have been made that way.

There are four main ways of making more plants: taking cuttings from existing plants, dividing clumps, layering stems, and sowing seeds. The method you use will depend on the plant, the time of year, and what is most convenient for you. It may also depend on the equipment you have. Often there are various options, since plants may propagate in several ways, so if you forget to sow seeds in spring, you may be able to take cuttings in summer.

Propagation methods

An easy way to propagate perennials and shrubs is by taking a cutting (see pp.114–35). This involves removing a part of the original plant (such as a section of a stem, a root, or a leaf) and putting it into potting mix or a jar of water; over time, roots will grow, and a new plant will form.

Where perennials form large clumps, these can be propagated by division (see pp.136–41). This involves dividing a clump into two or more sections, which can be planted elsewhere. The plants are garden-ready the moment you divide them, and will establish very quickly.

Some plants naturally produce tiny new plants (plantlets) at the end of stems still attached to the parent plant (see pp.144–47). By pinning down these stems (known as layering), you can encourage rooting; or, if the plantlet already has roots, it's simply a case of separating it from the parent and potting it to grow. Bulbs naturally produce new plants (offsets) around the base, and so they propagate almost by themselves (see pp.140–41).

Finally, perhaps the most exciting way to propagate is sowing seeds—particularly if you collect them yourself (see pp.148–57).

There are pros and cons of each propagation method. For example, seed sowing is likely to result in more new plants in a shorter time, but can be relatively high maintenance in terms of watering, light conditions, and pricking out. If healthy, disease-free parent plants are chosen, cuttings, divisions, and layering often need less aftercare. These will result in clone plants that are genetically identical to the parent, whereas not all seeds will resemble their parent.

Timing matters

Propagating the right plants at the right time gives you the best chance of success. In this chapter, I suggest plants that are particularly easy to propagate by each method. Any key time factors—when to take cuttings, how long plants take to germinate or root, or the best times to divide perennials—are also included.

A variety of propagation methods, clockwise from top left: taking a softwood cutting from a pelargonium; dividing a geranium by cutting through its crown and roots; gathering ripe gaura (*Oenothera linheimeri*) seeds to sow; and layering a wisteria in a pot.

TAKING CUTTINGS

An easy, reliable, and economical way of increasing your stock, taking cuttings enables you to create hundreds of new plants for free within a few months. There are various methods related to plant type and season, allowing you to propagate a wide variety of plants throughout the year.

Propagating plants from shoot-tip, stem, leaf, or root cuttings is much simpler than many people realize. It involves turning small offcuts of plant parts into rooted, shooted, leafing, and potentially flowering plantlets.

Types of cutting

The ripeness of a plant's stems is a key determining factor when it comes to deciding how and when to take cuttings. Softwood cuttings (see pp.122–25), as their name suggests, are taken from fresh, new shoots in spring or early summer; semi-ripe cuttings (see pp.126–29) are taken later in the season, usually from mid- to late summer and early fall; while hardwood cuttings (see pp.130–35) are taken from fully ripened shoots in late fall and winter.

While cuttings of most plants can be taken almost any time of the year during the growing season, some deciduous trees and shrubs are best propagated when dormant. For more specific advice, follow the step-by-step guides to each cutting type.

What makes a good cutting?

Cuttings produce exact clones of the plants they're taken from, so it's crucial to propagate

Left *Pelargonium* 'Pink Capitatum' grows well from softwood cuttings.

from healthy plants to avoid regenerating any diseased cells alongside healthy ones. Cuttings from healthy parent plants will also have a better chance of survival. Always select the most vigorous shoots from new growth. Non-flowering shoots are ideal, as a plant's energy stores have not been used up for its blooms.

Ideally, take your cuttings just before you plant them, and preferably in the morning rather than in the middle of a hot day, so that they don't dry out. It's worth taking twice the number of cuttings you need because not all of them will root. The amount of cutting material you take will depend on the plant and the type of cutting, so check the technique pages for each. Likewise, follow the simple steps relating to how and where to cut the plant for propagation—for example, just below a leaf node (where the leaf joins the stem) at the base of a softwood cutting. It's crucial to cut the part of the plant where growth cells are present, or the cutting will fail.

Storing cuttings

Although it's best to prepare and plant your cutting as soon as you can, it isn't always possible. If you have to wait before preparing your cutting, remove the lower leaves and insert the cutting in a jar half-filled with water, then place it in a cool, shady place, out of direct sun.

If you need to transport your cuttings (for instance, if you're taking a shoot from someone else's garden), you can store the cuttings temporarily in a plastic container, such as an ice-cream carton, rinsed with fresh cold water to increase humidity and sealed with a lid. Store the container somewhere cool and shady until you're ready to plant. For plants that dislike moisture on their leaves, such as lavender, rosemary, sage, and roses, avoid storing the cuttings in humid conditions and don't cover them.

Preparing the growing medium

To ensure their survival, cuttings need the best possible conditions and care throughout the rooting process. In most cases, you will be inserting your cuttings into a pot of potting mix, although for longer cuttings from woody stems, such as roses or hydrangeas, you may be planting them directly into a small trench in the open ground. Either way, it pays to prepare the growing medium well to promote rooting.

If you are planting cuttings in a container, fill the pot with propagation mix or a mix of 80 percent peat-free, general-purpose potting mix and 20 percent horticultural sand, to improve drainage.

If planting cuttings directly into the garden soil, select an area of the garden where the cuttings can grow undisturbed. Make sure that you choose a light, weed-free spot with free-draining soil, ideally out of direct sunlight, then dig a trench for the cuttings (see pp.130–31). Once planted (see the individual methods for planting information), water the mix or soil lightly.

Rooting preparations

Nature shows that it's perfectly possible to propagate plants using the growth hormone (auxin) that is already present in them. However, some people like to speed things up or increase their chances of success by dipping cuttings into synthetic auxin, commonly referred to as rooting hormone powder or gel. There are also some natural rooting powders containing seaweed. These do add cost, so weigh the benefits. I find that if cuttings are taken at the right time and kept in the right conditions, nature will do its thing without the extra expense.

Leaving cuttings to root

Cuttings from hardy plants can generally be stored outside over winter, provided they are placed in a sheltered spot where there is plenty of light, but not direct sunlight. Ideally, place them alongside a house wall or a shed, where it will be slightly milder. Light frosts will not harm the cuttings, but in places where temperatures fall to −20°C (−4°F) or lower, the plants will need to be moved under cover for protection, into a greenhouse, on a windowsill, or in a shed with some daylight.

Check your cuttings regularly. Do not let them dry out, but also don't overdo the watering or leave them standing in water. Too much moisture will result in cuttings rotting.

You can usually tell that young plants have rooted when you see roots coming out of holes at the base of the pot and new strong growth. Prior to this, you may see new growth, but cuttings often grow new shoots before the roots. They aren't necessarily ready yet, and should be left alone until the roots are visible.

A selection of new plants, clockwise from top left: a rooted hydrangea softwood cutting; rooted hebe cuttings ready to be moved to separate pots; gaura (*Oenothera linheimeri*) seedlings; a rooted rose ready to be planted in an individual pot and grown for another few months.

Repotting into individual containers

Once your cuttings have rooted, you'll need to give them more space to grow by repotting them into larger, individual containers filled with a richer potting mix (peat-free, general-purpose potting mix), increasing the size of pots gradually as the plants get larger (repotting). I tend to leave young plants in pots for about 6–12 months before planting them out in their final positions in the garden. This is because you can better control light levels and the growing medium without competition from other, more mature plants.

Watering and feeding young plants

You'll need to water your new young plants to make sure they don't dry out. However, make sure you don't overwater, to avoid swamping delicate root systems. Check the growing medium with your fingers and keep it just moist. Freshly rooted cuttings don't need feeding, but as young plants grow—about three or four weeks after being repotted—many will require more nutrients. Between spring and fall, I feed plants every 10–14 days with some general-purpose, balanced liquid feed or my own nettle feed (see pp.70–71). Be careful not to overdo the feeding, as too rich a diet can damage the roots of young plants.

Final planting and pinching out

If plants aren't fully hardy, wait until mild weather before planting them outside. Although plants are often tougher than we think, moving them from a very warm place, such as a greenhouse (especially if it is heated), directly to very cold ground can be too much of a shock. To enable the young plants to adapt gradually to their new environment before planting them outdoors, it's often best to harden them off by placing pots next to a house wall (where the temperatures are always higher than in the open garden), or in a sheltered area of the garden.

Keep an eye on your young plants and remove the tips of new shoots as they appear (see p.94). This stimulates the growth of sideshoots and reduces water loss while new roots are developing. The growth hormone (auxin) gets redirected to the lower part of the cutting, which helps the roots develop.

Left I use the shelter of the house to protect young plants. These cuttings are in trays for easy watering. In the winter I remove the trays to prevent waterlogging, but the plants still benefit from the slightly higher temperature beside the building.
Overleaf Swaths of lavender (*Lavandula* x *intermedia* 'Grosso') and the rambling rose 'Crimson Shower' are main features in my garden, all propagated from cuttings.

Softwood cuttings

Rooting more easily than any other type of stem cutting, softwood cuttings are usually taken in spring or the beginning of summer, soon after the shoots have burst into leaf and during a period of intense growth. Since the stems are soft and bendy, they tend to root relatively quickly, taking between two and eight weeks depending on the plant.

Softwood cuttings are usually taken from the top portion, or tip, of a shoot (as shown here), but they can also work with sections of stems cut from fast-rooting perennials. Most softwood cuttings should be cut just below the leaf node, where there is a concentration of hormones to stimulate growth. However, there are exceptions, such as deciduous clematis cultivars, which should be cut a little farther down the stem (about 2in/5cm) below a leaf node.

Here I'll show how to take a softwood cutting from lavender—one of my favorite plants. The same technique can be used to propagate most perennials and deciduous shrubs, as well as some trees, climbers, and annuals (see plant list, p.125).

You will need
Pruners, precision pruners, or scissors
Clean pot
Suitable growing medium
Watering can

1. Select a strong, healthy, nonflowering young shoot of the current season's growth. Using a clean, sharp knife or pruners, cut just below a leaf node (where the leaf joins the stem). Include at least two leaf nodes and cut to about 2–4in (5–10cm).

2. Remove the foliage, except for one or two pairs of leaves at the top. The surface area of large leaves can be reduced by cutting them in half to reduce moisture loss. Fill a container with propagating mix or a mix of 80 percent peat-free, general-purpose potting mix and 20 percent horticultural sand. Insert cuttings around the edge of the pot, to about two-thirds of their length and spaced 1–2in (2.5–5cm) apart (thicker stems need more space).

3. Water the potting mix. Place the pot in a sheltered, light site out of direct sunlight and leave the cuttings to root. Water them if they dry out.

4. Once the cuttings have developed a healthy root system and are growing well, pot them into individual containers.

1.

2.

3.

4.

A selection of plants growing from softwood cuttings, clockwise from top left: salvias reproduce readily from softwood cuttings; a hebe cutting rooted in a jar of water; softwood cuttings growing in pots; basal cuttings from lupins.

Suitable for softwood cuttings

Aster (*Symphyotrichum*)
Basil (*Ocimum basilicum*)
Cosmos
Dahlia*
Gaura (*Oenothera lindheimeri*)
Hebe
Hydrangea
Lavender (*Lavandula*)
Lobelia
Loosestrife (*Lysimachia*)
Lupin (*Lupinus*)
Penstemon
Phlox
Sage (*Salvia*)
Sweet pea (*Lathyrus odoratus*)
* *basal cuttings*

....

Anya's top tips

· Softwood cuttings are particularly prone to drying out, so water regularly to ensure the potting mix remains damp.

· If the cuttings are wilting, spray them with water and cover with a plastic bag or a cloche. However, there are exceptions: lavender, sage, rosemary, and roses should never be covered or sprayed with water.

· If seed from fast-growing annuals, such as sweet peas (*Lathyrus odoratus*) or cosmos, aren't germinating well, or become leggy, take softwood cuttings and put them into water. They should start to root in one or two weeks.

....

Rooting in water

Most softwood cuttings can root in water (as an alternative to potting mix)—a method that is particularly handy for fast-growing, leggy spring seedlings. Take a tip cutting in the normal way (see steps 1 and 2, pp.122–23), then place it in a glass jar half-filled with clean water so that roughly the bottom third of the cutting is covered. Place the jar in a light spot but out of direct sun, which could scorch the plant. If the water is in a warm, bright place, such as a kitchen windowsill, it can become cloudy. If that happens, simply pour it out, wash the pot or glass, and add fresh water. When healthy roots have developed (after about two to eight weeks), pot the cuttings into individual pots of potting mix in the usual way (see p.155).

Basal cuttings

Herbaceous plants with stems that become hollow, such as delphiniums, lupins, chrysanthemums, and dahlias, propagate better if cuttings are taken from the new spring growth at the base of plants in early spring. Select strong shoots 3–4in (7–10cm) long with the leaves just unfolding. Cut the shoots as close to the base as possible, then treat as for other softwood cuttings (see pp.122–23).

In the case of dahlias, one of my favorites, use a sharp knife to cut out new spring shoots (at least 4in/10cm long) with a small piece of tuber attached. Trim the lower leaves and insert cuttings into a pot of potting mix, leaving the top third of the stem exposed. Water, then store the cuttings at 61°F (16°C). Roots should appear after two or three weeks. Repot into individual containers and plant outdoors once all danger of frost has passed. You can also propagate dahlias by dividing tubers (see pp.140–41).

Semi-ripe cuttings

Mid- to late summer and early fall is the ideal time to take semi-ripe cuttings, when stems are still green and supple but have hardened at the base. You can propagate a wide range of plants using this method, including hardy perennials, climbers, trees, and shrubs—particularly evergreens.

Semi-ripe cuttings usually root in about three months if taken in summer, or up to six months if taken in fall. This is longer than for softwood cuttings, but semi-ripe cuttings tend to be more resilient.

The cuttings of woody plants root better if you remove a sliver of woody skin, prompting plant hormones known as auxins to heal the "wound" and then produce roots.

Here I'll show how to take a semi-ripe cutting from *Hydrangea arborescens* 'Annabelle'. Most types of hydrangeas are easy to propagate this way, except for *H. petiolaris* (propagate by layering, see pp.144–47) and *H. quercifolia* (grow from seed, see pp.148–57). See the list, right, for other suggested plants that you can propagate using this method.

You will need
Pruners
Sharp knife
Clean pot
Suitable growing medium
Watering can

1. Choose a healthy, vigorous, nonflowering shoot of the current season's growth, where the base is slightly woody but the tip is soft. Using pruners or a clean, sharp knife, cut just under a leaf node (where the leaf joins the stem).

2. Trim the cutting just above a leaf node at the top. Remove leaves from the lower third of the stem. If the plant has large leaves, cut off about one third of each to reduce the surface area. The final length of the cutting should be about 4–6in (10–15cm) long.

3. Fill a pot with propagation mix or a mix of 80 percent peat-free, general-purpose potting mix and 20 percent horticultural sand. Insert cuttings around the edge of a pot, to about two-thirds of their length and 1in (2.5cm) or more apart. Water the potting mix and place the pot in a light, sheltered spot out of direct sunlight, or in a cold frame.

4. Once the cuttings have rooted, pot them into individual containers. Pinch out each cutting to encourage it to grow sideshoots (see p.94).

Suitable for semi-ripe cuttings
Buddleia/Butterfly bush (*Buddleja*)
California lilac (*Ceanothus*)
Forsythia
Hebe
Lavender (*Lavandula*)
Nemesia
Pink (*Dianthus*)
Russian sage (*Perovskia atriplicifolia*)
Sage (*Salvia*)
Star jasmine (*Trachelospermum jasminoides*)
Rosemary (*Salvia rosmarinus*)

1.

2.

3.

4.

1.

2.

3.

4.

Taking a heel cutting

Heel cuttings are very reliable because the "heel," a tiny bit of bark that is pulled away from the stem, contains high levels of growth hormone. They are useful for perennials and shrubs that don't otherwise root easily. Heel cuttings can be taken as softwood, semi-ripe, and hardwood. Here I am taking heel cuttings from gaura (*Oenothera lindheimeri*).

You will need
Sharp knife
Clean pot
Suitable potting mix
Watering can

1. Select a plant that's growing strongly with plenty of new shoots.

2. Select a healthy, vigorous, nonflowering shoot of the current season's growth. Using a clean, sharp knife, cut a shoot from the stem about 2–4in (5–10cm) long. You can also pull it away if it's possible. Include a small tail or heel of bark at the base of the cutting.

3. Remove any leaves from the lower third of the stem. If the plant has large leaves, cut off about one third of each to reduce the surface area. Use a sharp knife to gently scrape the woody skin on semi-ripe or hardwood cuttings.

4. Fill a container with propagation mix or a mix of 80 percent peat-free, general-purpose potting mix and 20 percent horticultural sand. Insert cuttings around the edge of a pot, to about two-thirds of their length and at least 1in (2.5cm) apart. Water and place the pot in a light, sheltered spot out of direct sunlight, or in a cold frame. Once the cuttings have rooted, pot them into individual containers.

Suitable for heel cuttings

Dahlia
Delphinium
Gaura (*Oenothera lindheimeri*)
Lupin (*Lupinus*)
Penstemon

Anya's top tips

- For evergreen plants with large leaves, cut the leaf in half before inserting cuttings into potting mix to minimize moisture loss.

- Offer some protection to semi-ripe cuttings from the cold or waterlogged conditions over fall and winter by placing them in a greenhouse or a cold frame.

- Combine taking semi-ripe cuttings with pruning plants at the end of summer. Choose the strongest, healthiest stems for propagation, and they will produce a new batch of vigorous young plants by the following spring.

Hardwood cuttings

The main method of propagation for many deciduous climbers, shrubs, and trees (including fruit) is taking hardwood cuttings in late fall and winter, when the plants are dormant in the colder, darker months. Such plants can be expensive to buy as potted specimens or even as bare-roots, particularly if buying in quantity for hedging, so this is a great way to save money. The timing's good, as there's less to do in the garden at this time.

The cuttings take about four to six months to root. If taken in fall, you can leave them over winter and they should produce strong, healthy plants ready for the following spring.

You need to make two cuts for hardwood cuttings—one below a leaf node, the other above a leaf bud. The cuttings can be inserted into pots of growing medium (see overleaf), but large, robust cuttings can be inserted straight into a trench in the open ground, provided the area is fairly sheltered and light, but out of direct sunlight. For hardwood cuttings in a pot, see p.133. For an alternative, more economical method for roses, see pp.134–35.

I often use the trench method to multiply my own favorite roses (here, *Rosa* 'Crimson Shower') but also propagate wonderful new rose specimens from cuttings donated by friends. I save a lot of money that way because roses can be incredibly expensive to buy. The trench method is also suited to hydrangeas and other shrubs with large, thick stems.

You will need
Sharp knife or pruners
Spade
Horticultural sand (optional)
Watering can

1. Choose a firm, healthy shoot of the current season's growth (about the thickness of a pencil for roses). Using a sharp knife or pruners, make a straight cut just below a leaf node at the base. Cut off any sideshoots, then make a sloping cut just above a leaf bud at the top. The cutting should be about 6–8in (15–20cm) long.

2. Remove any lower leaves but leave one or two at the top if still in place. Using a sharp knife, gently scrape the woody skin off one side of the cleared section. This stimulates root formation.

3. Using a spade, dig a small trench in the garden about 8–12in (20–30cm) deep. If the soil is heavy, mix in a handful of horticultural sand to provide drainage.

4. Insert cuttings to about two-thirds of their length, about 4–6in (10–15cm) apart. Firm into position and water. There is no need to water again until spring; the ground should be sufficiently wet. The following spring, move the rooted plants to their final positions in the garden or pot them into individual pots (see p.135).

1.

2.

3.

4.

Rooted hardwood cuttings of roses starting to grow, all ready to be potted into separate pots. These cuttings were taken in late fall, and this image shows the growth the following spring.

Suitable for hardwood cuttings

Camellia
Cotoneaster
Deutzia
Dogwood (*Cornus*)
Escallonia
Forsythia
Hibiscus
Honeysuckle (*Lonicera*)
Hydrangea*
Philadelphus
Rose (*Rosa*)*
Spiraea
Tamarisk (*Tamarix*)
Viburnum
Willow (*Salix*)
can be planted in a trench

Rooting in pots

If you're taking only a few cuttings, or the cuttings are small, or growing space is limited, you may prefer to insert hardwood cuttings into pots. An added advantage is that you can have better control over a plant's growing environment. This method is particularly useful if you are moving and want to take precious roses or other shrubs with you.

Follow steps 1 and 2 on the preceding page, but make cuttings no more than 2–4in (5–10cm) long. Fill a container with propagation mix or 80 percent general-purpose potting mix and 20 percent sand. Insert cuttings to about two-thirds of their length and spaced about 1in (2.5cm) apart. Place the pot in a cold frame or unheated greenhouse, or stand it in a well-lit, frost-free, sheltered spot outside over winter.

An alternative way of taking hardwood cuttings of roses and rooting them in a pot is covered on p.134.

Root cuttings

Some perennials are better propagated by taking cuttings from sections of root rather than stems. These include verbascum, eryngium, echinacea (see image above) poppy (*Papaver*), and acanthus. Root cuttings are taken at the same time as hardwood cuttings, ideally in early winter during dormancy. Simply dig up a healthy parent plant, and remove one or two roots, using a sharp knife. Cut them into smaller sections about 2–4in (5–10cm) long, and insert into a pot of propagation mix. New roots and leaves will develop in spring.

Leaf node cuttings

This method is an alternative type of hardwood cutting, particularly suitable for roses of any type. Each cutting includes a leaf node, where the leaf grows out of the stem. These cuttings are smaller than regular hardwood cuttings, so you can produce more plants from a stem, making this method more economical. The cuttings also take a much shorter time to develop roots. Although the optimum time to take these cuttings is early spring, I've found they will also root until late summer.

You could use it for roses in your garden or those of a friend or neighbor, but it is also particularly useful for propagating roses given to you in a bouquet, or to make more plants from meaningful roses given as a wedding or anniversary gift.

You will need

Pruners
Planting tray
Peat-free general purpose potting mix
Horticultural sand
Larger pot

1. Cut a length of pencil-thick stem from a rose in early spring, just as the new leaves are starting to emerge. Ensure it includes one or more leaf nodes.

2. Divide the stem into small sections, about 1in (2.5cm) long, making a straight cut at each end of the cutting, and ensure each has a leaf node in the middle.

3. Place the cuttings horizontally in a tray containing a mix of peat-free general-purpose potting mix and horticultural sand. Place it outside in a sheltered area, perhaps next to a wall, but out of direct sun. Keep the soil moist.

4. The cuttings should develop roots after about 6–12 weeks. Transplant them to individual containers of rose potting mix or peat-free general-purpose potting mix.

....

Anya's top tips

- Don't take hardwood cuttings until flowering is over, and in most cases wait for deciduous leaves to fall off. This helps direct energy to where it is needed most. Avoid periods of severe frost.

- Always take more root cuttings than you need; some may not grow.

- Many cuttings take weeks or months to develop, so keep inspecting them and ensure they stay free of weeds and pests. Never place them in saucers if you're going away as they may become waterlogged, but you could use capillary matting so that they take up water slowly.

....

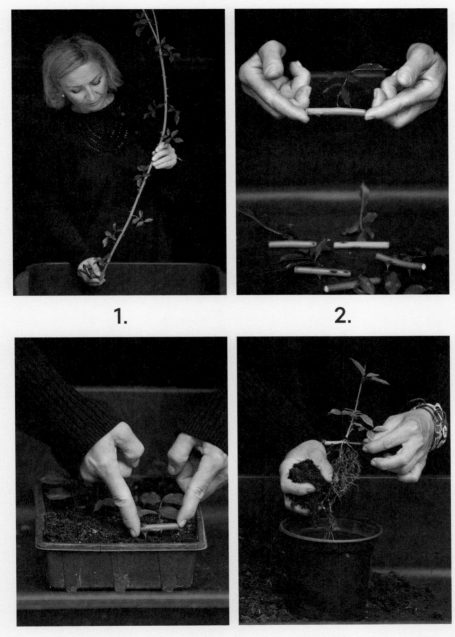

1.

2.

3.

4.

PLANT DIVISION

Dividing plants is an incredibly simple way of reproducing
two or more plants for the price of one, much more quickly
than by taking cuttings or sowing seed. Although it can work
for some shrubby plants, clump-forming perennials (see pp.138–39)
and bulbous plants (see pp.140–41) work best.

Division essentially involves digging up clumping plants, cutting them into two or more pieces, and replanting sections that will then grow into new plants that are identical to the parent. The best time for dividing is usually fall and spring.

Dividing for health and vigor

Many perennials need dividing every two to five years to keep them healthy, even if you don't want to propagate them. If left undivided, they can become overcrowded and will stop performing well—they may not flower as prolifically, can start to look tired and straggly, or may die out in the middle. Dividing perennials regularly rejuvenates mature, overgrown plants, helping them stay healthy and vigorous.

Dividing and replanting

When dividing plants, try to choose a day when the soil is damp. Alternatively, water the plant a few hours before you lift it. Dig it out and divide it into smaller pieces where the roots divide naturally. The way you split the clump depends on the plant. Smaller plants that form low-growing clumps, such as snowdrops (*Galanthus*), primulas, and heucheras can be very easy to divide, and once dug up sections can simply be pulled apart by hand. Those that form a tight mass of rootstock, such as peonies (*Paeonia*), astilbes, and agapanthus, are much harder to separate. In many cases you'll need cutting tools, such as a sharp knife, a garden fork, a spade, or even (rarely) an axe, to divide the clump. Try to be careful, but don't be scared of division. Plants are very accommodating and most will respond well to whatever you do.

Ideally, plant the divisions right away so that they don't dry out. Larger divisions can be planted directly in the garden, ideally in small groups, while smaller divisions or larger divisions that can't be planted outside right away can be potted into individual pots of general-purpose, peat-free potting mix. Water well to keep them moist.

Left The astrantia and geranium 'Rozanne' in this border have both been propagated by division.

Dividing perennials

The perennials most suitable for division are clump-forming plants, and the method for dividing these is shown here. Non-clumping perennials that have a single taproot that grows straight down into the soil, such as lupins (*Lupinus*), various poppies (*Papaver*), and wallflowers (*Erysimum*), are hard to divide because they have compact growth that does not spread out. These plants are best propagated by cuttings (see pp.122–25), or seed sown in a pot (see pp.152–55).

Generally, it's best to divide clump-forming perennials in spring, when plants enter a period of rapid, strong growth, or in fall, while the ground is still warm. The process relies on a section of root being left on each division to support new growth. Although divided clumps are smaller than the parent, they soon expand into a space.

Some plants have specific requirements, so it's best to research them carefully. For example, primulas benefit from division right after flowering, whereas peonies should be divided in fall after five years and left alone for five years before dividing again. Peonies must be planted no deeper than 2in (5cm) and spaced 20–30in (50–75cm) apart if planted in groups.

Here I'm dividing a clump of hardy geraniums (*G.* 'Rozanne'), which are super-easy to divide. This technique can be used for many other perennials (see plant list, right).

You will need
Garden fork
Spade
Dividing tool, such as a knife or spade
Potting mix
Watering can

1. Select a healthy specimen for division and water well a few hours before lifting if the soil is dry. Select a new planting area, fork over, and add garden soil or other organic matter. Then dig a hole large enough to comfortably take the roots of your division. Carefully dig up the parent plant, leaving as much soil as possible around its roots.

2. Closely examine the plant and decide where to make your divisions. Separate the leaves to see how the clumps are growing and aim to cut between clumps.

3. Divide the plant. Here, I'm using a sharp knife, but you may need to use a spade for tougher roots, or you may be able to use your fingers to pull them apart. You can repeat the process if you want more, smaller divisions.

4. Replant the divisions immediately to avoid the plants drying out. Backfill the hole with a soil and compost mix, firm, and water well.

Suitable for division
Aster (*Symphyotrichum*)
Astilbe
Astrantia
Bellflower (*Campanula*)
Catmint (*Nepeta*)
Feather grass (*Stipa*)
Geum
Heuchera
Hosta
Moor grass (*Molinia*)
Pearly everlasting (*Anaphalis*)
Rudbeckia
Saxifrage (*Saxifraga*)

1.

2.

3.

4.

1.

2.

3.

4.

Dividing bulbous plants

Plants with underground food storage organs, including bulbs, corms, tubers, and rhizomes (often known simply as bulbs), frequently produce small plantlets (offsets) around the main plant. Since offsets are also able to root and shoot as complete plants, they can be dug up, divided, and replanted. Many spring-flowering bulbs, such as snowdrops (*Galanthus*, shown here), grape hyacinths (*Muscari*), and crocuses, are most easily divided after flowering, while the leaves are still visible. This helps plants restore vitality by easing congestion, while also saving on buying bulbs next year.

You will need
Garden fork
Labels
Watering can

1. Just after flowering, carefully dig up a clump of bulbs using a garden fork. Remove any excess soil. You should notice main bulbs with clusters of small bulblets (offsets) at their base.

2. Divide the clump into smaller clumps by gently teasing the roots apart with your hands. Try to keep a few bulbs together; snowdrops, like many other late winter and early spring favorites, look better in groups.

3. Replant the offsets into well-drained, prepared soil at the same depth as before—in separate pots, in mixed containers, or in the ground. Label their position.

4. Once planted, water them, then let the foliage of repositioned bulbs die back naturally to recharge their storage organs.

Other division methods

Plants with thick, horizontal stems that creep at or below ground level, such as many irises and ginger, are called rhizomes. They respond well to division, usually in spring. Detach new, healthy rhizomes from the clump and use a sharp knife or spade to cut the rhizome into sections, each with a bud and some roots. Replant in well-prepared soil improved with organic matter and a little horticultural sand, ensuring that new buds are just below the soil surface. Firm and water well.

Tubers are swollen roots, such as dahlias, which are among my favorite plants. I divide clumps of tubers each spring before growth begins to flower the same year. Divide each clump into sections using a sharp knife, or pull apart "hugging tubers" by hand. Each division must have at least one healthy growth bud ("eye"). Plant the divisions about 5in (12cm) deep, with the growth bud uppermost and in their final flowering positions, after all danger of frost has passed. You can also take basal cuttings of dahlias in early spring (see p.125).

Suitable for division

Allium
Begonia
Crocosmia
Daffodil (*Narcissus*)
Dahlia
Day lily (*Hemerocallis*)
Fritillaria
Grape hyacinth (*Muscari*)
Nerine
Ranunculus
Siberian iris (*Iris sibirica*)

LAYERING PLANTS

One of my favorite methods of propagation, layering is an extremely quick and easy way of reproducing a wide range of popular shrubs and climbers, as well as some perennials. Layering happens naturally in our gardens, and we as gardeners just lend a helping hand.

When a low branch of a shrub or climber touches the soil, it can take root and produce a new plant (plantlet or offset). In some cases, the new plant remains attached to the parent, while in others the connection is severed, leaving an entirely independent plant. Layering simply mimics this natural process by burying part of the stem in the ground, anchoring it down, and waiting for it to root.

One key advantage of layering is that the parent plant "looks after" the layered stem while it's rooting, so the new plant doesn't need any additional care (although adding organic matter and horticultural grit to the soil can help). Then you just wait for the magic to happen!

When and how to layer

Layering is usually done in spring or fall for deciduous plants, although if layered in fall, nothing will happen until the following spring. Evergreens are better layered in spring. Simple layering works for many plants (see plant list, right, and method on pp.146–147) but air layering (see p.147) is another option. In both cases, you need to scrape away a section of bark to prompt growth hormones to stimulate root formation.

Some plants root very quickly in two to four weeks, while others—including wisteria and climbing roses—can take up to a year.

Viburnum and hydrangeas root very easily on their own. If this occurs naturally in your garden, simply remove the offset by cutting it away from the parent plant once it is showing some growth, and plant it elsewhere.

Suitable for layering
Acer*
Azalea*
Camellia*
Clematis
Climbing hydrangea (*Hydrangea petiolaris*)
Climbing and rambling roses (*Rosa*)*
Daphne*
Dogwood (*Cornus*)
Flowering quince (*Chaenomeles*)*
Ivy (*Hedera*)
Jasmine (*Jasminum*)
Lilac (*Syringa*)*
Magnolia
Rose (*Rosa*)*
Smoke bush (*Cotinus*)*
Strawberries (*Fragaria*)
Viburnum*
Wisteria
also suitable for air layering

Right A rooted wisteria, produced by layering in a pot. **Previous pages** Two prolific dahlias: pale pink 'Gurtla Twilight', and the deeper salmon pink 'American Dawn'.

1.

2.

3.

4.

How to propagate by simple layering

This method works for most plants that can be propagated by layering, including wisteria (shown here). Although wisteria takes a long time to root—about 12 months—and may not produce flowers for the first couple of years, it is a good investment plant and will deliver over time. It's well worth the wait.

You will need
Sharp knife
Pot of 80 percent general-purpose potting mix and 20 percent horticultural sand (optional)
Galvanized metal wire
Watering can

1. Select a flexible, vigorous stem of the current year's growth that will bend down to a pot or to the ground. Using a clean, sharp knife, scrape about 1in (2.5cm) of bark from the underside, where the stem is going to be in contact with the soil, cutting to a depth of no more than 1⁄16in (2mm).

2. Bend the stem into the soil, and where the wounded part touches the soil, make a hollow about 2in (5cm) deep, and bury the cut area.

3. Secure the stem with strong, galvanized metal wire looped over to prevent it from being displaced, or put a rock or a brick on it.

4. Water, and keep it moist over the next few months, reducing watering in winter. After six months, test whether your new plant has rooted by pulling gently on the end of the stem. Resistance indicates rooting. Once rooted (see p.145), it can be cut from the parent and planted outdoors.

Air layering

This is a useful technique for layering plants with stems that can't be bent to ground level, such as camellias. The layering takes place on a shoot higher up the plant and off the ground.

In early spring, choose a straight shoot about one or two years old, and trim off any leaves and sideshoots to leave about 12in (30cm) of clear stem. Make a sloping upward cut into the stem just below a leaf node (where the leaf meets the stem), forming a tongue. Pack potting mix around the stem and into the cut, dampen, and wrap a small plastic bag around the wounded area. Tie it tightly at either end to seal. Leave the plastic on for about a year to enable the stem to root into the potting mix. When strong roots have formed, remove the plastic (see below), and cut the young plant away from the parent.

GROWING FROM SEED

Seeds are some of the most amazing phenomena in nature, with the power to create multitudes of new plants, often from microscopic beginnings. As well as being exciting and rewarding, growing from seed—with its potential for seed-saving and swapping—is ideal for increasing your stock of ornamental and edible plants for free.

Nowadays, seed-sowing usually starts with a packet, but it's easy to get carried away when buying packs of seeds, and costs soon add up. Instead, I prefer to collect seed from plants in my garden or from friends' plants, or to join seed swaps (see p.151). It's a fun, self-sufficient way of growing more plants for free, with no negative impact on the environment. Growing freshly collected seed is often more successful than using dried, bought seed.

I find the process of saving and sowing what our garden provides is a wonderful way to connect with the cycle of life. The plant's main purpose is to survive and reproduce, and there I am, holding the potential for this new life in the palm of my hand—it's incredible! Gardening in harmony with nature—at nature's own pace—is also therapeutic, slowing us down and teaching us patience as we wait for the flowers to produce their harvest, then wait for the seeds we have collected to start on their journey to becoming fully fledged plants. Although nature's pace is slower than buying a plant at a nursery, seed sowing can make a huge impact within just one season, producing robust, flowering plants of many kinds.

There is a wide selection of seeds that can be collected through the year (see p.151), but it's important to note that not all will grow into plants that are "true to type," meaning that they resemble their parent plant. This may be because the parent plant cross-pollinated with another variety, or simply because the resulting seeds are weaker than the one that the parent grew from. That doesn't mean you shouldn't experiment. Gardening is an adventure and not everything goes to plan; that's what makes it exciting. The plant you grow from collected seeds may not come true to type, but it could be that something else entirely new and wonderful has been created in the process.

Suitable for seed saving
Achillea
Erigeron (*Erigeron karvinskianus*)
Foxglove (*Digitalis*)
Gaura (*Oenothera lindheimeri*)
Hellebore
Honesty (*Lunaria annua*)
Honeywort (*Cerinthe major*)
Poppy (*Papaver*)

Right I like to blow the dandelion-like seeds of yellow salsify (*Tragopogon dubius*) to help them self-seed in the meadow in my garden.

Collecting seeds, clockwise from top left: seeds from the papery seed cases of honesty are best sown direct right away to flower the following year because it doesn't like being moved; seeds of love-in-a-mist (*Nigella*) can be collected once the seedhead is ripe; seeds from Mexican daisy (*Erigeron karvinskianus*) can be sown right away or the following spring; poppy seeds need to be sown direct as they don't like to be moved.

How to collect and store seeds

Always give seeds enough time to ripen on the plant. If collected too early, they won't germinate. Watch carefully for flowers to turn brown, and wait for a dry day. You can then either break open the seedpods to extract seeds and put them in an envelope or paper bag, or (if they don't come out easily) cut off the whole stem and shake the seeds into a bag. Alternatively, put the stem upside down in the bag, seal it, and hang it in a dry, airy place, so that the seeds drop into the bag. Separate seeds from other debris or "chaff" (a sieve can help with this).

Consult a reputable guide for instructions about sowing, germination, and harvest times for the particular plant you're planning to grow. Some seeds need to be sown right away, such as buttercups (*Ranunculus*), hellebores, clematis, anemones, and delphiniums, while others need storing for winter or spring sowing. Many seeds, especially from shrubs or trees, germinate faster if they're chilled before sowing, and certain seeds—including sweet peas (*Lathyrus odoratus*)—tend to germinate more quickly and reliably if they're soaked in warm water first. Seeds with hard cases, such as lupins (*Lupinus*), may benefit from cutting or scratching (scarifying) the surface to allow moisture in, necessary for germination.

How to save seeds

If you're going to store seeds rather than sow them right away, place them in a paper bag or envelope, and keep them in a dry, cool place out of direct sunlight. Air circulation is essential for most seeds—any mold or moisture and the seeds may be spoiled.

Always store seeds from different plants in separate bags, and write the name of the plant on the bags and ideally also the date you collected the seed; otherwise you're likely to forget what's in them. Some seeds naturally last longer than others, even if they're stored in the optimum conditions, so research their viability and ensure that you don't go past their "sow by" date, or they will have a much lower chance of germination.

Seed swapping

Once you start saving seeds, you may quickly find yourself with huge amounts of a particular variety that you'll never have the time or space to sow. Instead of letting this surplus go to waste, why not set up a seed swap with friends, family, or neighbors? Some local areas advertise more organized seed swaps, too. That way, you can share your yield with others while introducing new plants into your garden to keep things interesting.

Sowing seeds in pots

Many seeds can be started off indoors in pots, seed trays, and modules much earlier in the season than if sowing outdoors—some even in fall. As well as being protected from the weather, plants sown indoors are easier to look after than those sown direct into the garden.

If you're new to seed sowing, or want an easy ornamental or edible fix, choose plants with large seeds such as nasturtium, sweet peas (*Lathyrus odoratus*), or zucchini. Small, light seeds—such as strawflowers (*Xerochrysum bracteatum*) and snapdragons (*Antirrhinum*)—can't be sown individually due to their size. Instead, sieve a thin layer of potting mix over the top. Stand the pot in a container of water until the surface is damp, to keep from washing them away while watering.

I haven't listed plants suitable for sowing in pots as almost all seeds are suitable for this, apart from those that don't like to be transplanted (see p.157). Use the containers that you have, and scatter the seeds or sow them individually depending on the seed size. Here I show you the basic method of sowing, pricking out, and transplanting using a variety of seeds, taking them from seedlings to small plants in the garden. For more detail on how to prick out and transplant, see pp.154–55.

Basic sowing guidelines

Fill a pot or module with fresh, peat-free seed starting mix or a mixture of 50 percent general-purpose peat-free potting mix, and 50 percent horticultural grit. Level the soil and lightly water. Large seeds can be inserted individually into the mix, spaced some distance apart to give them space to grow and reduce competition. In a 3½in (9cm) pot, insert just one or two seeds per pot. For fine seeds, you need to scatter a thin layer of seeds over the surface of the seed-starting mix. Cover the seeds with a layer of mix (ideally sieved) until they are completely covered. Water the seeds carefully; for fine seeds, stand the pot in a container of water until the surface is damp, to keep from washing them away while watering. Label each pot, then place it on a bright windowsill or in a greenhouse. Prick out the seedlings when they emerge (see p.154).

Anya's top tips

- Ensure the surface of the mix is level when sowing so that the water doesn't wash the seed to one side.

- Some seeds, such as primulas, poppies (*Papaver*), busy lizzies (*Impatiens*), and eccremocarpus, need light to germinate, so leave them uncovered when sowing.

- If you're growing lots of seeds, it may be worth investing in a simple bottom-heat propagator to place on a windowsill. I find it really makes germination more successful.

From seed to flowering plant, clockwise from top left: collecting hellebore seeds from a dried seedpod; a flowering hellebore plant; sweet pea seedlings growing in cardboard tubes; sweet peas in flower.

Pricking out seedlings

When the seedlings have developed two or more sets of leaves and are large enough to handle, the most robust need carefully transplanting, or pricking out, into individual pots. If you've sown two or more seeds in a single pot, module, or tray, you will need to pull out and discard the weaker seedlings to give the strongest ones more space to grow properly without being crowded out by their neighbors.

It's best to work with small batches of seedlings so that they don't dry out, and water the plants about an hour or two before you start. Use a pencil or stick to loosen the soil among the seedlings, then gently tease out weaker plants and dispose of them. Fill several pots with propagating mix or general-purpose peat-free potting mix. Ease out larger seedlings with soil around their roots. Make a small hole in the center of each pot. Holding each seedling gently, lower it inside the hole to the same depth as it was in its original container. Gently firm the potting mix around the roots, water lightly, and label. When you've done the whole batch of seedlings, place the pots in a bright place out of direct sunlight.

Hardening off

Tender plants need acclimatizing before planting outside in a process called hardening off. This involves putting plants in a sheltered spot outside during the day for a short time, then extending the time that plants are outside over the course of a week or two, until they're staying out all day and eventually nights too, covering them with horticultural fleece or reused packing material for the first few nights.

Planting outdoors

Once the seedlings are considerably larger, with several sets of leaves, and danger of frost has passed, it's time to plant your seedlings out in the garden. First, prepare the soil, removing any weeds and raking it into a fine tilth, then water the area to be planted. Ensure the seedlings are spaced to the correct distances apart for the plant you're growing. They will quickly develop extensive root systems and bushy top growth. If there's any chance of frost, cover with horticultural fleece or newspaper to help trap the sun's warmth. You may also need to consider pest and disease control (see p.76) to help prevent losing precious plants.

Right pot, right plant

Ensure any pots used are clean and have good drainage holes so that seedlings don't get waterlogged, which can rot roots. Also, choose the right pots for specific seeds. Sweet peas, for example, have long roots and therefore need longer root trainers. It's easy to use the cardboard center of a toilet paper roll for these (see p.153).

Growing seedlings, clockwise from top left: checking trays of seedlings after germination; pricking out a seedling, carefully lifting it from a tray of seedlings; firming an individual seedling into its own pot to grow; a seedling grown in a module, ready to be planted into a bigger pot or out into the ground to grow.

Sowing seed directly into the ground

Sowing directly where possible saves time and money; it's also vital for plants that don't like to be transplanted, such as carrots, parsnips, and other root crops; herbs with long taproots such as parsley; and flowering plants such as honesty and poppies. You can sow in rows or scatter seeds more evenly in drifts, known as broadcasting. The soil should be prepared by removing weeds, digging, and raking to a fine texture. Some plants may need added organic matter such as manure or compost.

You will need
Seeds
Label
String
Rake
Watering can

How to sow seed in rows
For me, sowing in rows is for the vegetable and cutting garden. It offers the most efficient way to sow as many seeds as possible, with easy access to weed and harvest. The seeds can be sown into rows where they are going to grow.

1. Using a stick and string to keep the rows straight, make indented rows in prepared soil about ¾in (2cm) deep (the finer the seed, the shallower the row needs to be). Rows should be about 12in (30cm) apart.

2. Place two seeds at regular intervals within the row—check for the optimum sowing distance for the seed you are sowing. Cover the seeds with a thin layer of soil, gently tamping it down to firm it. Water the soil gently.

1.

2.

How to broadcast sow

This method is used mainly for sowing annuals in a border, where seed is scattered randomly to create a natural, informal effect. Here (see left, below), I am gathering and broadcasting yellow rattle seeds (*Rhinanthus minor*), which are perfect in a meadow (see pp.50–53).

1. Collect seeds from their seed pods.

2. Scatter the seeds around. If you're scattering on bare soil, lightly rake them in, then water.

Suitable for direct sowing

Annual clary (*Salvia viridis*)
Blue lace flower (*Didiscus caeruleus*)
Marigold (*Calendula officinalis*)
California poppy (*Eschscholzia californica*)
Flax (*Linum*)
Honesty (*Lunaria annua*)

Lace flower (*Orlaya grandiflora*)
Love-in-a-mist (*Nigella damascena*)
Erigeron (*Erigeron karvinskianus*)
Night phlox (*Zaluzianskya ovata*)
Night-scented stock (*Matthiola longipetala*)
Opium poppy (*Papaver somniferum*)
Rose campion (*Lychnis coronaria*)

Anya's top tips

- Thinning ensures strong, healthy plants. Remove weak seedlings to avoid overcrowding, thinning to the final distance (check your seed packet for this information).

- When thinning vegetables such as lettuce, you can eat the thinnings.

1.

2.

PROPAGATING SUCCULENTS

A number of succulent varieties are very easy to propagate, creating hundreds of new plants each year from just one specimen. There are several methods that can be used (see below), and the process can be done inside or outside, at almost any time of year. Once the cuttings have developed into young plantlets, they can be used to create a fun display for a sunny spot (see pp.172–73), or gifted to friends and family.

There are a few methods for propagating succulents. Here, I'll be focusing on leaf propagation, using rosette-forming varieties such as the relatively hardy echeveria or the fully frost-hardy hen and chicks (*Sempervivum*) or some stonecrops (*Sedum*).

You can take just a few leaves from near the base of the plant, but if you want to create a lot of plantlets, it may be worth breaking down a whole mature plant. If you can't bear to do this to a healthy specimen, head to the reduced section of a homeware shop or garden center, and see if you can find any in need of rescue.

You will need
Tray
Stick
Seed-starting mix or general-purpose peat-free potting mix, mixed with sand

1. Select a mature, healthy leaf on your parent plant. Carefully pull it to one side so that it "pops" off the stem; roots will only form from the leaf's base. Repeat as needed.

2. Fill a tray (with drainage holes) with peat-free potting mix or seed-starting mix. Mix in a little sand for extra drainage. Insert the leaves into the surface so that their bases are in contact with the potting mix. Water gently and place in a sunny, sheltered spot.

3. Leave the tray until a new plant has formed at the base of the leaf, keeping the mix moist but not saturated. Some leaves will begin to produce roots, followed by small rosettes. Remove any leaves that shrivel up.

4. When the plantlets are large enough to handle, use a stick to carefully lift them from the soil. The parent leaves may fall away at this stage, or can be gently snapped off. The plantlets are now ready to plant.

Anya's top tips
- If you have to transport your succulent leaves before planting them (for instance, if you've been given some from a friend), wrap them in newspaper rather than in a plastic bag, as they do not like humidity.

- Succulents are drought-tolerant and low maintenance. It's far better to water too little than to give them too much to drink.

1.

2.

3.

4.

CHAPTER 6
A YEAR IN THE GARDEN

For me, creating a garden is like writing a theatre script. You want the audience to be entertained through the whole show—through every season. With a little planning and imagination, the script comes together, leaving your star performers—your plants— to perform at their best.

SPRING

New beginnings bring so much excitement. Seeds are germinating, seedlings are growing, and the bees are starting to fly around looking for some early spring flowers. It's a busy time, so aim to plan and be selective about how you spend your time. But make sure you stop from time to time to enjoy the spring flowers along the way.

As winter draws to a close and the days start to grow a bit longer, I'm eager to spend more and more time in the garden. Every year I like to try something new, whether its a new variety of seed to sow or a new location for plants. This is what I love about gardening: you always learn.

The seed-sowing season

I start sowing as many seeds as I can from early spring. Spring is the best time to sow seed for many beloved plants, including annuals like zinnias and cosmos, and biennials including forget-me-nots, foxgloves, honesty, sweet William, and wallflowers. Leave sowing of more tender plants until a bit later in spring so that they will be ready to plant outdoors once the frosts have passed.

Unpredictable weather

Recent years have shown us how rapidly our climate is changing, and we need to adapt in our gardens. Sowing and other forms of propagation can be a buffer against the unpredictable weather that we are increasingly experiencing—and against the more usual challenges of spring, when sharp frosts, deluges of rain, or conversely very dry months all need to be factored in.

If you choose more resilient plants and sow or grow cuttings of plants that you could potentially lose in more extreme weather, you can be one step ahead of what is happening, and have plants ready to replace any that you may lose.

Jobs for spring

- Create plant supports ready for sweet peas and other plants using branches you have saved when pruning (see pp.166–69).
- Repot any plants that have outgrown their space, or replace the top layer of potting mix if they are too big to transplant.
- Check young plants for slugs and snails (see p.76).
- Plant evergreen trees and shrubs, and any bare-root plants (see pp.83–84).
- Mulch beds to suppress weed growth and add nutrients to the soil (see p.69).
- Trim hedges and ornamental grasses, and edge your borders.
- Make your own fertilizer (see pp.70–71).
- Divide summer-flowering perennials as they start growing, and snowdrops straight after flowering (see pp.136–41).
- Layer plants (see pp.144–47).
- Take heel (see p.128) and basal cuttings (p.125) from dahlias, lupins, and delphiniums.
- Propagate by softwood cuttings from spring until early summer (see pp.122–125).

Chive hedge

Chives are one of those hardworking super herbs: they add visual interest to your garden, they taste great, and their flowers are loved by pollinators and have a very long vase life when used in floral arrangements. They work well in pots or on a windowsill, but do best in the ground. Combine multiple seed-sown chive plants (or make the most of a few supermarket-bought pots) to create a mini-hedge—an ideal feature to border a path or flower bed.

In my garden, I'm very selective, mainly opting for plants that are multipurpose and aren't too fussy. Chives (*Allium schoenoprasum*) check all the boxes. Happy in sun or partial shade, and easily rejuvenated in midsummer with a simple chop, they are also low-growing—to about 12in (30cm)—so they won't cast much shade on other plants. The early spring, pink-purple, nectar-rich blooms of chives help feed a range of pollinators, and the plants come back year after year. They work in even the smallest space.

In this project, I've used a mix of chives I've grown from seed (see pp.152–55), which I started off in early spring, and their supermarket counterparts. Chives from seed are excellent value, producing many plants that last for years. Supermarket herbs are a great option for time-pressed gardeners, often costing a lot less than similar offerings in garden centers. These densely packed pots have a reputation for not lasting long, but there is a solution—see step 2, right.

You will need
Chive seeds or plants
Pot or tray
Suitable potting mix
Watering can
Trowel

1. If you're growing your own chives from seed, start them off in early spring by sowing a pinch of seeds into a pot or small tray filled with a mix of potting mix and horticultural sand. Water well and place on a warm windowsill indoors to encourage germination, then move them outdoors to harden off for at least a few weeks (see p.154). Once the plants are around 4in (10cm) tall, they are ready to plant outdoors.

2. If using supermarket-bought chives, carefully lift the whole "plant" from its pot; you will find that you actually have a number of smaller plants grown together. Tease the rootball apart into 2 or 3 pieces.

3. Using a trowel, dig a hole deep enough for the chives' roots. Place the first chive into the hole and firm it into place. Continue to plant more chives along the line of your hedge, spacing them 10in (25cm) apart. Water the plants in place.

4. The chives will soon begin to fill the space. They may not flower the first year, but should do so the following spring. It's a good idea to divide chives every 2–3 years to keep them performing well. This will give you even more plants for elsewhere in the garden, or to gift to friends and family.

1.

2.

3.

4.

Sweet pea obelisk

Sweet peas (*Lathyrus odorata*) are one of the joys of summer, filling the garden and vases with sweet-scented flowers and, depending on the variety, a riot of color too. Maximize their impact by weaving your own growing frame using just a few sturdy branches and plenty of pruned stems.

While they may look complicated, obelisks are surprisingly easy to construct, and instantly create impact in a garden. Once you've made a few, they can take under an hour to assemble, especially if you have someone to help you. I recommend using hazel sticks—you may be able to get some from a local coppicing company. Birch or wood from other trees you have available is also suitable, but avoid willow or dogwood, which may root. A well-made obelisk will last for a year or two, but will eventually need to be replaced as the stems dry out and become brittle.

Sweet peas are best sown (see pp.152–55) in spring or fall in deep, narrow pots, though repurposed toilet paper tubes are also ideal for their long roots. Fall-sown ones tend to be more robust and bushy, and will usually flower earlier than those sown in spring. They are hardy and will overwinter except in the coldest conditions. For my favorite sweet peas, see the list on p.169. If you keep cutting the flowers, you should have buckets of blooms to use at home, to sell, or to swap with others.

You will need
Assortment of large and small branches
Loppers or a pruning saw
Garden twine
Sweet pea plants

1. Gather 6–8 large branches, and an assortment of thinner, flexible stems. Cut the large branches so that they are an equal length; I like to cut them to be around 6ft (2m) long, so that the finished obelisk stands at around my height, making it easier to cut sweet pea flowers later. I use a sloping cut at the base so that it has a point that is easier to stick into the ground.

2. Push the straightest branch into the middle of the spot where you want the obelisk to stand, and tie a length of twine about 20in (50cm) long to the base. Tie a small stick to the other end of the string. Use the stick to trace a circle around the central branch.

3. Insert the remaining large branches into the ground at equal points around the circle. If the branches are curved, position them so that they arch inward.

4. Fold a length of string in half and hold it in one hand. Gather all of the branches together around the central branch (you may need a helper for this!), and then draw the doubled-over string around them. Thread the ends of the string through the loop and pull tight, then wind it back over itself several times and tie the ends together to hold the branches secure.

1.

2.

3.

4.

5.

6.

7.

8.

5. Twist together any thin shoots emerging from the branches, gently bending them slightly downward and around the obelisk. Begin to introduce your thinner, flexible stems into this twist one at a time, creating a kind of "rope" to loop around the obelisk.

6. When the rope crosses a branch, open up the stems into two bunches, so that one crosses in front of the branch and the other behind. Twist the two bunches back together on the other side of the branch.

7. Let the rope of thin branches curve naturally around the obelisk, inserting more flexible stems and weaving in any other branch shoots you encounter. Continue until you reach the base.

8. Plant a sweet pea seedling at the base of every branch, and tie each one to the support to give it a start. As they grow they will twine naturally up and around the obelisk (right). Mulch with grass cuttings (see pp.68–69).

Sweet pea favorites
'Blue Velvet'
'Earl Grey'
'Erewhon'*
'Lisa Marie'
'Matacuna'
'Memories'*
These Modern Grandiflora varieties have large flowers; long, strong stems; and excellent scent

SUMMER

To keep your garden looking its best, it helps to stay on top of its growth, trimming, deadheading, supporting, and harvesting fruits and flowers. This gives you a chance to get to know how your plants grow, plus you get to see some of your garden wildlife up close, from bees, butterflies, and other pollinators to toads hiding in the shady corners.

Early to midsummer is the time when I give myself a break to enjoy "the show." I take it in with all my senses, walking around the garden and observing how everything is growing. I do this for two reasons. First, I do it to celebrate the fruits of my labors: to see the flowers in bloom and to marvel at the growth of any newly planted seedlings and cuttings. Secondly, it helps me, as a money-conscious gardener, to make a note of what is growing well—and what isn't.

Plants really have to work hard to be here in my garden, and by watching and writing it all down, I can make plans for next year. Yes, I'm already thinking about next year! I recommend keeping a notebook and writing down your observations, and taking plenty of photos that you can look back on during the quiet winter months (see pp.180–83).

Time out

It can be hard to leave your garden in summer, but if you do go away, ask a neighbor or friend for help and let them harvest your vegetables and pick some flowers in return.

Temperatures rising

Our summers are getting hotter, and it makes sense to rethink your plant choices and go for drought-tolerant varieties, especially for containers. Those plants will perform with minimum effort but will give you maximum result. Gaura and Mexican daisy (*Erigeron karvinskianus*) are just two examples; see pp.172–73 for more drought-tolerant plants. Mulching pots with straw or wool sheets (recycled packaging material) is a good idea to save water, keep pots weed free, and protect plants from slugs.

Jobs for summer

- Prune lavender after flowering.
- Stake any plants that are growing too tall and are struggling to stay upright.
- Deadhead flowering plants daily to encourage more blooms.
- Trim the edges of lawns with a half-moon edger to keep beds and borders neat.
- Feed flowering plants with a high-potash fertilizer, such as comfrey (see pp.70–71).
- Direct sow seeds including foxgloves and honesty (see pp.156–57).
- Propagate softwood cuttings of shrubs and perennials in early to midsummer (see pp.122–25).
- Propagate semi-ripe cuttings from mid- to late summer (see pp.126–29).
- Prune summer-flowering shrubs in late summer.

Use what you've got

Rise to the challenge and use only self-propagated plants and repurposed containers to create eye-catching displays that cost absolutely nothing. Of course, you can reuse an old plant pot, but where's the fun in that? Get creative by repurposing household items: boots, colanders, saucepans, or even beloved childhood toys, as I have done here.

Depending on the container you choose, you can create interesting plantings of edibles and ornamentals, flowers and grasses, or perennials rather than annuals for a long-lasting, return display. It's also a good way to encourage year-round propagation so that you have a ready supply of free plants to play with.

This toy dump truck first belonged to my husband, and then my sons. Now a little worn out, it was very nearly thrown away—until I rescued it and gave it a new life as a container for my propagated succulents. Here I'm using varieties of echeveria succulents propagated from leaves (see pp.158–59). Whatever item you want to repurpose, make sure it has drainage holes (the dump truck has a handy gap along the base); if it doesn't, carefully add a few, to reduce the risk of waterlogging, which will damage (or even kill) the roots.

You will need
Repurposed container
Reused plastic sheeting
Scissors
Potting mix
Sand
Stick for handling plants
Self-propagated plants

1. Line the base of the container with repurposed plastic sheeting (an old potting mix bag, for example), cut slightly smaller than the container itself so that it doesn't rise over the sides. Puncture it in several places to allow for drainage.

2. In a separate container, mix together potting mix and and. As I am planting succulents, I've added half sand and half potting mix; adjust this ratio depending on the needs of your chosen plants (see p.16). Add this to your chosen container, leaving ½–1in (2–4cm) below the rim.

3. Gather your propagated plants. With a stick, gently tease and lift a plant from the growing container, taking care not to break the roots. If the plant is still connected to the leaf it was propagated from, cut this away with scissors. Make a small hole in the potting mix in your chosen container and add the plant. Once all plants are added with space to grow, cover any exposed soil with a layer of sand to aid drainage around the leaves.

4. Water your plants regularly so that they establish well, and particularly during dry spells. They should slowly grow and spread to cover the potting mix. Echeveria is not hardy, so I take this container inside over the winter. If you use hardy succulents such as sempervivum or *Sedum album*, you can leave your container outside all year.

1.

2.

3.

4.

1.

2.

3.

4.

Tumbling tomatoes

Growing your own fruit and vegetables is great fun, and gives you a cheap source of fresh produce. Cherry tomatoes, particularly "tumbling" varieties, are very fruitful and ideal for smaller gardens and balconies because they can be grown in containers or hanging baskets. Add some attractive, naturally pest-busting companion plants for a colorful and sustainable summer display.

We used to grow hundreds of tomato plants (*Solanum lycopersicum*) in our greenhouse when I was a child. The scent of the leaves is particularly evocative and reminds me not just of the plentiful round, red fruits of our labor—eaten straight from the plant or added to meals—but also that absolutely nothing got wasted.

I recommend buying seed when growing tomatoes for the first time. This guarantees the best possible quality and disease resistance, which in turn gives you the best chances of a good harvest. 'Tumbling Tom Red', a compact, tumbling variety with a height and spread of around 12in (30cm), is ideal for small spaces, and doesn't need staking or pinching out. After your first harvest, save seed for next year, and you'll have an annual tomato crop for free!

You will need
Tomato seeds
Pots or trays
Peat-free potting mix
Watering can
Suitable container
High-potassium plant food

1. Sow seeds into pots or trays of peat-free potting mix in spring, sowing more seeds than the number of plants you expect to need later. Water well and place somewhere warm, sunny, and sheltered to germinate, such as a windowsill or greenhouse.

2. When the seedlings are large enough to handle, prick out and transplant the strongest into individual 3in (9cm) pots. Continue to keep young plants inside until all danger of frost has passed. When the weather begins to warm up, bring the plants outside during the day for around a week to acclimatize.

3. Find a sunny, sheltered spot for the tomatoes' final growing position. Fill your chosen container with peat-free potting mix and add two or three plants, leaving plenty of room for them to grow. I'm using a hanging basket lined with a coconut fiber liner on the outside, plus a layer of plastic from an old potting mix bag inside, with a few small holes for drainage.

4. Keep the plants well watered as they grow. Once flowers appear, feed with fruit-boosting, high potassium comfrey feed (see pp.70–71). Fruits will develop later in summer, provided that the plants are visited by pollinators. Pick tomatoes as they ripen.

FALL

The days may be getting shorter and the garden may be about to go to sleep, but there is still plenty for gardeners to enjoy—and make the most of—in fall. As trees shed their leaves, vegetable patches offer up their harvests, and flowering plants put on their last show of the season. This is a season of color, joy, and opportunity.

Colorful leaves, berries, and bark are fall highlights, but it's also a time to notice whether your garden is lacking in color and to make a note of plants you like that could add some extra interest at this time of year. Ornamental grasses can come into their own in fall, in addition to a range of fall-flowering shrubs and bulbs.

Bargain hunting

Everyone loves a good end-of-season sale, and fall is a great time to grab a bargain from garden centers, who may need to shed stock before the quieter months, or have a surplus of summer-flowering favorites to sell off. Head for the clearance section, often tucked away in a quiet corner, and you may find real treasure. Spring bulbs, for instance, may be marked down in late fall, once their "proper" planting season has passed, but if you plant them as soon as you can, they should be just fine. Alternatively, take a chance on some tired-looking perennials; by next year, they'll bounce back to life.

Elsewhere in the garden center, now is the best time to pick up trees, shrubs, and roses. Buy bare-root specimens, which are far cheaper than those sold in pots. Again, plant them as soon as you can when you get home because fall is the ideal season to establish new trees and shrubs (see pp.83–84).

Fall leaves

If you or your neighbors have deciduous trees, fall brings with it a rainbow of fallen leaves. Resist the temptation to clear them all away. Leaves that have fallen on bare soil will break down over winter, providing nutrients and replenishing the ground beneath. Undisturbed leaf piles also provide much-needed shelter for wildlife over winter months: places for creatures to hibernate or hide while so much of the land is bare. If you do need to clear leaves from paths or lawns, they can be added to the compost heap, or left in sacks for a year or so to create leafmold mulch. Nothing is wasted.

Jobs for fall

- Prune later-flowering lavenders in very early fall; if pruned after that they may be damaged by early frost, so it's better to leave it until spring.
- Keep propagating from semi-ripe cuttings (see pp.126–29).
- Divide perennials and irises; peonies can be divided only in fall.
- Sow sweet peas (see pp.152–55).
- Harvest seeds from some seed heads, leaving the rest to feed birds and other wildlife over winter.
- Plant spring-flowering bulbs.

Pot of joy

Planting spring-flowering bulbs and corms in fall is a great way to promote successive seasonal interest in the garden. Visualizing the end results also brings hope and positivity to get you through the colder, darker months. Plus, bulbs can be great value for the money especially if they're bought later in the season, or acquired as offsets from plants that you already have.

For my fall-planted pot of joy, I've chosen my favorite tulip, *Tulipa* 'Danique', a perennial variety that will flower year after year, but you can experiment with a wide range of bulbs and corms. You could spread the joy even further by making a bulb lasagne, layering up successive spring and summer blooms. This is a quick and easy project that will pay dividends the following spring.

You will need
Large pot
Peat-free potting mix
Horticultural sand
Bulbs of your choice
Watering can

1. Choose a pot with drainage holes that will suit your end display. Add peat-free potting mix, mixing in some horticultural sand for extra drainage. Don't pack the potting mix down firmly at this stage.

2. Arrange the bulbs pointed-side-up on the surface of the potting mix, keeping them 2in (5cm) apart so that the blooms have room to flourish later. Press them into the potting mix slightly so that they stand in place.

3. Once you're happy with the arrangement of the bulbs, press them into the soil so that they are buried to a depth of three times their height; in the case of my 'Danique' tulips, this is 3.5in (9cm).

4. Firm the potting mix over the top of the bulbs, cover with horticultural sand, and water the pot. Place in a sheltered spot, ensuring that the potting mix remains moist but not waterlogged over winter. By spring, green shoots will appear, signaling the start of the new season to come.

1.

2.

3.

4.

WINTER

The quietest season in the garden can still be a busy one for gardeners. With little to do outside, winter is the time for reflecting on what worked well over the preceding growing season—and for making plans and ordering seeds for the year ahead. There is plenty to think about as the new year dawns, from the plants you want to propagate to the changes you want to make.

One of the best things to do in your garden in winter is to let it be. Leaving stems and seedheads of perennials gives beneficial insects places to shelter and hibernate over the winter, and birds will feed on the dried seeds. They will deal with slugs and snails in early spring.

Out and about

Winter is a great time for visiting public gardens and gathering ideas. Creating year-round interest is a challenge, but it's a skill that can be learned from the expert gardeners who tend these open spaces. I've found that buying a ticket for a public garden teaches me far more than a horticultural course—and costs far less, too. This is how I learned to create plant supports (see pp.166–69).

Take note as well of what draws your interest in these winter gardens: the trees and shrubs with textured bark or evergreen leaves, the bulbs that are starting to emerge, and the flowers that linger on into the cooler, duller months. Write it all down, take pictures, note the names—then take it all home to add to your research and planning for next year.

Winter interest

If the garden is your stage and winter is the final act, you don't want to end on a dull note and have your audience fall asleep. Yes, the garden may slow down as temperatures drop, but our gardens still have so much to offer in winter. Invest in statement plants that offer winter and early spring interest, and they'll pay you back by providing much-needed interest: I personally love hellebores, Algerian iris (*Iris unguicularis*), *Hepatica*, the climber *Clematis cirrhosa*, and *Erica cornea*. And, when flowers are relatively few, it's worth focusing on other areas of interest, like the textured bark of *Prunus serrula*, which looks magical when catching some late afternoon sun or meeting the frost, or the fiery-colored stems of dogwoods (see pp.182–83). With a few well-chosen additions, there's no reason for the garden not to grab your attention, even in the depths of winter.

Jobs for winter

- Order seeds for next year (if you were unable to collect your own in fall; see pp.148–51).
- Take hardwood cuttings of fruit and ornamental shrubs (see pp.130–35).
- Take root cuttings of plants such as echinacea and verbascum (see p.133).
- Keep pruned branches to use as plant support in the spring.
- Store tender plants in a frost-free environment.

Dogwood display

You can bring winter color closer to home by making your own decorative display from foraged branches and foliage combined with winter-blooming plants. Bright red dogwood (*Cornus*) branches saved after pruning can be given a second life as an eye-catching, low cost display over the colder months.

Dogwood branches are a true winter highlight, beloved for the vivid stem color they bring to the darker winter months. Not only do they look great planted in beds en masse, but their pruned stems can also be used to create a fiery explosion of color that lasts through winter and well into spring. Moreover, once you're ready to dismantle the display, some of the cut branches will have rooted over the winter, giving you new plants for the spring, while those that haven't can be used as supports for sweet peas and other plants.

As with so many money-saving gardening tips, timing is the key. Dogwoods need to be pruned in late winter or early spring, to encourage new jewel-colored shoots to form the following fall and winter. Right after pruning is the time to create this display.

You will need
Pruners
Container
Reused potting mix from pots, or peat-free potting mix
Other winter plants (optional)

1. In late winter or early spring, prune dogwoods down to 6–8in (15–20cm). If you don't have any dogwoods in your own garden, ask a friend or family member for their prunings (or offer to do the job yourself) to gather your supply of stems, or ask the gardeners at a local park or public garden.

2. Find a container at least 8in (20cm) deep, with drainage holes. Fill the pot with leftover potting mix from old pots, or soil from mole hills (see p.69). Use new potting mix if you don't have old. Insert the first stem at least 3in (8cm) deep, or until it feels secure. Add a few more stems at intervals around the edge of the container to create an even, balanced effect.

3. Continue adding stems to achieve an effect you're happy with, until the whole container is filled. If you don't have enough to completely fill the container, you can also plant winter favorites, such as winter cyclamen and hellebores, which will grow up through the stems and add an extra layer of interest.

4. In spring, when the branches have faded, it's time to remove them. Check, by pulling each one gently, whether it has rooted. Transplant any rooted cuttings to a new position to grow.

1.

2.

3.

4.

BRINGING IT ALL TOGETHER

As you work through a year in the garden, you'll gradually change your mindset and establish your own money-saving routine by working with the seasons and using what you already have. Your garden is a place for you to experiment, explore, learn, and have fun—and all of it can cost next to nothing if you follow a few simple guidelines.

It doesn't matter how large or small your growing space is. Even on a balcony or a windowsill you can apply the same principles and just adjust the scale. Everyone can create an amazing garden without breaking the bank.

Making the most of plants

As you develop a more frugal, resourceful mindset, you'll think twice about which plants to buy and how many boxes they check to maximize value for money and results in the garden. To be more mindful about spending will become second nature as you experience the rewards of spending less while creating something beautiful and unique. Buying expensive plants in flower will become a thing of the past because you'll have many of the plants you like already in your garden and it'll be free to create more. You'll want to try different propagation techniques and discover more plants and combinations.

You'll quickly learn how to garden in a more self-sufficient, sustainable way. Nothing that grows in your garden will go to waste. Nettles will be turned into precious nitrogen-rich fertilizer, grass cuttings will form a mulch, and hedge trimmings will be put to use as plant supports.

Working with nature

Observing nature and working with it rather than against it saves a huge amount of money, and offers great enjoyment. So much less effort and equipment is needed if you do things at the right time because you'll have nature on your side. Propagation helps you understand how plants grow—you are making the most of their natural drive to survive and reproduce. By filling your garden with a variety of plants, you are helping to create and strengthen an ecosystem that will support you in return. If your garden provides food, shelter, and a home for wildlife, the wildlife will help to regulate less desirable garden visitors that might nibble your plants. You'll get to see every day how nature sustains your garden.

Being resourceful

Repurposing, reusing, thinking outside the box, and propagating will save you a fortune and you'll create a resilient and healthy garden at the same time. It's also a garden for the future: adaptable, sustainable, and beautiful. My watchwords are minimum effort and maximum result: I hope that you can achieve the garden of your dreams, too, by following some of the simple methods in this book.

RESOURCES

Recommended books

The following books are a great investment for any money-conscious gardener. They are all well worth buying, but you could also see if your local library has a copy to borrow.

Encyclopedia of Garden Plants **edited by Christopher Brickell, 4th edition (DK, 2014)**
This truly is my bible. Every gardener should have this book. The most reliable source of information about garden plants.

Pruning and Training **by Christopher Brickell and David Joyce (DK, 2017)**
Everything you need to know about pruning over 800 plants.

Containers in the Garden **by Claus Dalby (Cool Springs Press, 2022)**
This is a fantastic source of inspiration that can be easily translated into money-saving gardening. The use of perennials, even mixing them with ornamental vegetables, is truly innovative in this book.

Grow Food for Free **by Huw Richards (DK, 2020)**
A great book for cost-conscious gardeners who want to grow their own food and get more for their money.

Propagating Plants: **edited by Alan Toogood (DK, 2019)**
This book is a must-have for anyone who would like to understand more about propagation, with over 1,500 different plants featured.

Websites

Royal Horticultural Society (RHS)
rhs.org.uk
There is no better place for me than the RHS website. Always up to date, it includes everything that a gardener needs.

Pinterest
pinterest.com
I often use Pinterest in the winter just to feed my mind with ideas. It's a great place for money-saving gardeners who are looking for inspiration.

National Wildlife Federation
nwf.org
A great source of information on how to make your garden a wildlife-friendly place.

The Xerces Society for Invertebrate Conservation
xerces.org/endangered-species/butterflies
A nonprofit organization that protects the natural world through the conservation of invertebrates and their habitats, including butterflies.

INDEX

laurel 47
lavender 18, **18**, **26**, 64, 73, 87–8,
    171
  French 88
  propagation 111, 116, **119**,
      122–3, 125–6
  pruning 88, 171, 177
lawn mowers 35
lawns 50–2, **50**, **53**
  edges 36, 44, 171
  grass pathways 44, **44**
  length 50, 63–4
  watering 73
  weeds 50
layering 83, 111–12, **113**, 144–7,
    163
  air layering 147
leaf mold 69
leaves, fallen 64, 177
lichen 44
light levels 16, **18**, 39, 87, 96
lilac 144
  California 126
lily 99
loam 16
lobelia 125
London pride 104
loosestrife 125
love-in-a-mist **18**, **56**, 93–4, **95**,
    150
lupin **42**, **124**, 125, 129, 138, 151,
    163

M
magnolia 144
manure 18, 40, 69, 87
  green 40, 70, **75**
marigold 64, 94, 157
mazus, creeping 44
meadows 50, **50**, 52, **53**, 63–4, **65**,
    99, 106, **148**, 157
meadowsweet 23
mindful gardening 11, 15
molehills 69
moor grass 138
morning glory **46**, 96
moss 44
moths 64, **75**, 93

moving plants 24, 39, 84, **84**
mulching 29, 35, 64, 66–9, **69**, 73,
    84, 87, 163, 185
muscari 100, **100**, 141
mustard, white 70

N
nasturtium 64, 152
nature 63–4, 111, 148, 185
nemesia 126
nerine 100, 141
nettle 63, 70, 88, 185
new gardens 26
nitrogen 66, **67**, 70, 88
  fixation 50, 70

O
obelisks, sweet pea 166–9
offsets 112, 141, 144
organic matter 24, 26, 29, 39–40,
    69–70
oxygenators **54**, 55

P
parsley 156
parsnip 156
passionflower 96
paths **42**, 43–4, **44**
patios **42**, 43–4
pearly everlasting 138
Pelargonium **113**
  P. 'Pink Capitatum' **115**
penstemon 125, 129
peony 48, 80, 137–8, 177
perennials 79, 87–8, 96, 102–4,
    107, 181
  buying 80, 177
  choice 87
  companion planting 64
  drought-tolerant 73
  herbaceous 79, **89**, 125
  planting 26
  propagation 40, 88, 122, 125–6,
      137–9, 163, 171, 177
pesticides 64, 74
pests 63–4, 74, **75**, 100
petunia 94
Phacelia tanacetifolia 70, 75

philadelphus 133
phlox 44, 103, 125
  night 157
pinching out 94, 119
pink (*Dianthus*) 126
planning 15, 26, 39–40, 80
plant health 74, **75**
plant supports **29**, 48, **49**, 84, 96,
    96, 166–9, 171, 181, 185
plant understanding 77–107
planting outdoors 26, 35, 84, 100,
    119, 154
plantlets 112, 141, 144
plastic 11, 57
"plug" plants 80
pollinators 64, 102–3
ponds **54**, 55
poppy **72**, 73
  California 157
  opium 94, 157
  propagation 133, 138, 148, **150**,
      152, 156–7
pricking out 154
primula 137–8, 152
privet 47
propagation **11–12**, 11–12, 57, 80,
    102–7, 109–59, **111**, 185
  by season 163, 171, 177, 181
  climbers 96, 122, 126, 144
  ground-cover plants 44
  growing mediums 116
  hedging plants 47
  methods 112, **113**
  perennials 40, 88, 122, 125–6,
      137–9, 163, 171, 177
  shrubs 83, 126, 144
  timing 112
  see also cuttings; division;
      layering; seed-sowing
protecting plants 18, 116, **119**,
    154, 181
pruners 36, **37**
pruning 84, 94, 129, 163
  hedges 47
  lavender 88, 171, 177
  shrubs 23–4, 48, 84, 171
  tools for 36
trees 48, 84

water violet 55
watering 84, 119
weather 163
weed killers 50–2, 64, 69
weeds 35, 64, 69
wildflower meadows 52, **53**, 63–4, **65**, 99
wildlife 47, 50, 63
  habitats 47, 63, 177, 181
willow 133, 166
willow moss 55
winter 181–3
wisteria 96, **113**, 144, **144**, 146–7
witch hazel, common 23
woodchippings 29
worms **17**, 69

Y
yarrow (achillea) 103, 148
yellow rattle 52, **53**, 157
yew **46**

Z
zinnia 163
zucchini 64, 152

Author acknowledgments

I dedicate this book to my mum who, by introducing me to propagation over 30 years ago, started a real passion in me, and to my mother-in-law who sadly passed away before I could tell her about this book, but who inspired me on so many levels. She would have been proud and I'm glad I propagated her garden before her time came to an end. Her legacy lives on in my herbaceous borders and in this book.

I would like to heartfeltly thank my boys Richard, William, and Edward for their love and for inspiring me every day. You are my world.

My very grateful thanks goes to Chris Young who gave me an incredible opportunity, and to the most amazing team at DK: Amy Slack, Barbara Zuniga, Ruth O'Rourke, Maxine Pedliham, along with my incredible photographer Britt Willoughby-Dyer, editor Jane Simmonds, and designer Nikki Sims. You are all simply the best!

A massive thank you to my dear friend Katy Dunn for believing in me years ago and asking me to write for 'Clarion', our parish magazine.

A big shout out to my lovely friend and floral maestro Claus Dalby. You are my inspiration!

Love A.

Publisher acknowledgments

DK would like to thank Polly Boyd and Sonya Patel Ellis for initial editorial work, Francesco Piscitelli for proofreading, and Lisa Footitt for indexing.

Anya Lautenbach is a self-taught gardener with a passion for the environment and championing neurodiversity. She grew up in Poland, and after traveling for many years in Germany and the Scottish Highlands, she now lives with her husband and two sons in Buckinghamshire, UK, where her garden has blossomed through years of propagation and clever gardening tricks.

Anya's lifelong passion for nature and for propagating plants inspired her to share her knowledge to her followers across social media. There, as Anya the Garden Fairy, she provides easy-to-follow tutorials covering a range of accessible and achievable gardening techniques, and reveals tips and tricks for creating high-impact, low-cost gardens that work in harmony with nature. Anya also uses her platform to raise awareness about neurodiversity and the positive influence that horticulture can have on mental health. She proves that gardening does not need expensive equipment or specialized training—anyone can transform their garden and create something truly amazing.

You can find Anya online at:
Instagram: @anya_thegarden_fairy
Facebook: @anya_thegarden_fairy
Tiktok: @anyathegardenfairy
Youtube: @anyathegardenfairy
Website: www.anyalautenbach.com

Penguin Random House

Editorial Manager Ruth O'Rourke
Project Editor Amy Slack
US Editor Lori Hand
Senior Designer Barbara Zuniga
Senior Production Editor Tony Phipps
Production Editor David Almond
Senior Production Controller Stephanie McConnell
DTP and Design Coordinator Heather Blagden
Sales Material & Jackets Coordinator Emily Cannings
Art Director Maxine Pedliham
Publishing Director Katie Cowan

Editorial Jane Simmonds
Design Nikki Ellis
Consultant gardening publisher Chris Young

First American Edition, 2024
Published in the United States by DK Publishing
1745 Broadway, 20th Floor, New York, NY 10019

DK a Division of Penguin Random House LLC
24 25 26 27 28   10 9 8 7 6 5 4 3 2 1
001–336741–Feb/2024

Published in Great Britain by
Dorling Kindersley Limited

ISBN: 978-0-7440-9234-9

Printed and bound in China
www.dk.com

MIX
Paper | Supporting responsible forestry
FSC™ C018179

This book was made with Forest Stewardship Council™ certified paper – one small step in DK's commitment to a sustainable future. **For more information go to** www.dk.com/our-green-pledge